The Story of the
Declaration
of
Independence

The Story of the
Declaration
of
Independence

by Ira G. Corn, Jr.

CORWIN BOOKS
Los Angeles

Photo Credits (for 32-page photo section)

Page 1: Courtesy Library of Congress. Pages 2, 3, 4, 5: courtesy New York Public Library Picture Collection. Page 6: UPI. Page 7: *Thomas Jefferson,* painting by Charles Willson Peale, *c* 1791, courtesy The Independence National Historical Park. Page 8: Courtesy New York Public Library Picture Collection *Thomas Paine,* painting by John Wesley Jarvis, *c* 1805, courtesy National Gallery of Art, Washington. Gift of Marian B. Maurice. Page 9: Both courtesy New York Public Library Picture Collection. Pages 10 and 11: patrick Henry's "Parson's Cause" Speech. Painting, courtesy The Virginia Historical Society. Pages 12 and 13: Courtesy New York Public Library Picture Collection. Page 14: John Hancock. Detail of painting by John Singleton Copley, oil on canvas. Painted 1765, courtesy Museum of Fine Arts, Boston, deposited by the City of Boston. *Benjamin Harrison,* courtesy Library of Congress. Detail from painting, *Declaration of Independence,* by John Trumbull, in the United States Capitol. Page 15: *William Whipple,* painting by Ulysses D. Terry after John Trumbull, courtesy The New Hampshire Society of Colonial Dames. *Stephen Hopkins.* Courtesy Library of Congress. Detail from painting, *Declaration of Independence,* by John Trumbull, in the United States Capitol. *Robert Treat Paine,* painting by Edward Savage. Courtesy Charles J. Paine. *Roger Sherman,* painting by Ralph Earle. Courtesy Yale University Art Gallery, New Haven. Page 16: *Philip Livingston,* painting by Benjamin West. Courtesy Mrs. John Henry Livingston. *Robert Morris,* painting by Charles Willson Peale, courtesy The Pennsylvania Academy of Fine Arts, Philadelphia. *John Witherspoon,* painting by Charles Willson Peale, *c* 1783, courtesy Princeton University, Princeton, N.J. *George Read,* painting by Robert Edge Pine, courtesy New York Public Library Picture Collection. Page 17: *Samuel Chase,* painting by Charles Willson Peale, *c* 1773, courtesy Maryland Historical Society, Baltimore. *William Hooper,* courtesy Library of Congress. Detail from painting, *Declaration of Independence,* by John Trumbull, in the United States Capitol. *Edward Rutledge,* courtesy New York Public Library Picture Collection. *Francis Lightfoot Lee, Edward Rutledge, Lyman Hall,* all courtesy New York Public Library Picture Collection. *John Dunlap,* painting after Rembrandt Peale, courtesy First Troop Philadelphia City Cavalary Armory, Philadelphia. Page 19: courtesy Yale University Art Gallery, New Haven. Page 20: *Congress Voting Independence,* engraving by Edward Savage, *c* 1796-1817, courtesy The Massachusetts Historical Society. Page 21: Courtesy New York Public Library Picture Collection. Page 22: Richard Henry Lee's Resolution, manuscript, courtesy National Archives, Washington, D.C. Page 23: Courtesy New York Public Library Picture Collection. Page 24: *Harper's Monthly,* July 1853, courtesy New York Public Library Picture Collection. Page 25: *Harper's Monthly,* July 1851, courtesy New York Public Library Picture Collection. Pages 26 and 27: Courtesy Library of Congress. Pages 28 and 29: Courtesy New York Public Library Picture Collection. Page 30: Courtesy of author. Page 31: Courtesy Library of Congress—UPI. Page 32: Courtesy of author.

THE STORY OF
THE DECLARATION OF INDEPENDENCE

Published by
CORWIN BOOKS
One Century Plaza
2029 Century Park East
Los Angeles, California 90067

Dedication

To my Mother
MARTHA VICKERS CORN
Whose love of books and appreciation
of history I inherited

To my Father
IRA G. CORN
Whose sense of discipline and responsibility
has guided me throughout my life

Acknowledgments

This tribute to the Declaration of Independence could not have been written without the support and assistance of Joseph P. Driscoll, co-owner with me of the "Lost Copy,"; Andrew Ettinger, Editorial Director of Pinnacle Books, Inc., whose idea it was for me to write the book; and Dorothy Moore, whose valuable criticism was helpful in shaping much of the material.

My special thanks also to Frederick R. Goff, former Chief of the Rare Books Division of the Library of Congress, who provided many of the details concerning the John Dunlap Broadside and the First Printing of the Declaration of Independence.

Special credit should go to the Library of Congress for its 1976 publication entitled, "First Printing of the Declaration of Independence."

And, finally, my thanks to Connie Hardison for typing the manuscript and to Floyd Wood for special editing assistance.

IRA G. CORN, JR.
Dallas, Texas
February 1977

TABLE OF CONTENTS

Introduction

Personal freedom, our most precious and distinct possession, is enjoyed by Americans to an extent unrivaled elsewhere, even in "free" societies such as Canada and England.

Dr. Milton Friedman, the Nobel Prize winner, frequently points out that five thousand years of man's recorded history have been written in tyranny and misery. This means that it has been accepted as normal throughout history for personal freedom to be restricted and affluence scarce. Less than one percent of the people who have lived on this planet have known the concept of personal freedom, and those who lived in the few societies that provided some personal freedom usually were severely restricted.

For example, during Plato's time the Greeks used the Republic as a model for a living, successful democracy. What is seldom mentioned is that this democracy applied

1

only to twenty percent of the people. The remaining eighty percent were slaves. Similar conditions existed in the Roman Empire except that the number of citizens, as opposed to slaves, was far less than twenty percent.

In England the Magna Carta was a proclamation against the tyranny of the king on behalf of a very small class, the barons. Virtually no personal freedom was attained until the invention of the printing press. Freedom is an extension of knowledge that soon became more widely disseminated. Gradually people realized what they were missing. They also learned that people were similar and that the concept of aristocracy by birth was a myth perpetuated by the nobility, or ruling classes.

Visualize, if you will, a gigantic screen filled with a million plugged-up holes. Each plug in this screen represents a barrier to extending personal freedom to all members of society. When all of the holes are plugged, freedom does not exist. Through the centuries some of these holes were opened, such as at the signing of the Magna Carta. Until the time of the Declaration of Independence more than ninety percent of the holes were still filled, even in an advanced society like that of England's, which offered more freedom in the eighteenth century than any other society in the world. But that freedom bore little relationship to that found in the United States today.

In one political document of approximately three thousand words, the concept that it was possible to unplug most of the holes in that screen was first proclaimed. That document was the Declaration of Independence. Two hundred years later, the challenge remains to remove more barriers to personal freedom and thus unplug more holes. The Constitution itself, adopted in 1791, had many plugs. Only men were allowed to vote, and only then if they owned property; the institution of slavery was tolerated in part of the nation; citizens had no vote in the se-

2

lection of senators—that choice was left to the state legislatures. Obviously, freedom was not handed to the early Americans in a completed form. It is a process of continuing growth requiring the efforts of all of us.

When people see the possibility of possessing an elusive dream such as freedom, they tend to become more and more aggressive in the pursuit of that dream. As some persons were given the right to vote, others demanded it. In recent times, more barriers that had prevented millions of citizens from voting have fallen.

The due process clause of the Constitution is probably the single most effective statement in American law that protects personal freedom. It makes it impossible for an authoritarian government to restrain a citizen without going through due process to the satisfaction of the courts.

Government, whether dictatorship or democracy, has always been reluctant to accept criticism from its people. It may be possible to keep people in absolute submission, but when government starts releasing them from submission, it is releasing a flood that cannot be stopped. The effort to attain personal freedom is a continuing battle to unplug holes in that gigantic screen. All of the holes will never be unplugged. Total freedom can never be attained. Imperfections, followed by steps to remedy them, are continually being brought to the attention of society. But the United States has unplugged more of those holes than any country in the world. And the Declaration of Independence is history's most important document toward the realization of maximum personal freedom for all members of an organized, orderly society founded on equal justice for all.

Some people today claim that such emphasis on personal freedom is unreasonable. They say the American people enjoy a privilege that is unjustified and undeserved. They also claim that freedom is more of an illusion than a fact. Alexis de Toqueville, in his early nineteenth-century book, *Democracy in America,* commented that the potential danger to United States democracy was that eventually the politicians would learn to buy the people and the people would be willing to be bought. This observation, made 140 years ago, is thought by some to be coming true today.

In reading about the Declaration of Independence, I have felt that the psychology of the times, the hundreds of incidents leading up to the drafting of the Declaration, and the reception it received have never been properly presented. I refer to the emotional impact of history upon those who conceived the Declaration of Independence, the reasons why they wrote it in a particular fashion, and its effect on the subsequent writing of the Articles of Confederation. The argument that the Articles of Confederation were inadequate led to their revision, which, in turn, formed the basis for the Constitution and the Bill of Rights.

It is important to understand the influence of the writings and beliefs of many important persons who lived in the 150 years prior to the Declaration's approval. One of the early thinkers was John Locke who, while living in England, expressed views that in many respects were the forerunners to many ideas expressed in the Declaration of Independence. It is not generally known that he also influenced ideas written in the constitution and the bill of rights for one of the colonies while employed as secretary to Lord Shaftesbury in London. During the seventeenth and eighteenth centuries various United States colonies passed constitutions and bills of rights. While these varied, of course, from the one eventually approved for the United States, the concept of such documents preceded the Declaration of Independence by more than three quarters of a

4

century. The colonists from time to time added principles derived from their own experience over the decades.

Contrary to the broad claims in the Declaration, the British colonies in North America were treated with generosity and fairness in comparison with colonies owned by other nations. In the sixteenth and seventeenth centuries American colonists gradually perceived how productive personal freedom was. This idea did not exist anywhere else. Certainly the colonists appreciated the productiveness of their society, but there was also a feeling that since the colonials were developing the cities, towns, and the natural resources, they, not England, should be entitled to the benefits.

The colonists were anxious for England to defend them against the French during the French-Indian War, but they were reluctant to pay for the troops, supplies, and arms. This dispute was used to justify demands for expansion of their personal freedom, which led to throwing off the mother country. Personal freedom became even more precious with each passing decade of the eighteenth century.

In some respects the dispute over the cost of defending the colonies was a question of where the decision was made rather than what was decided. Because the decision was made in London that certain troops should be maintained to defend the colonies, the colonies argued that the decision was wrong. If the decision had been made by the colonies they may very well have come up with the same answer. England was also unfortunate in the royal selection of several governors who unnecessarily provided frequent and ample opportunity for criticism.

The development of personal freedom in the colonies paralleled the Industrial Revolution in England in its latter stages, particularly after 1750. The use of English common law as it applied to the "law merchant" involved

5

the law of partnerships and negotiable instruments. The law, in the colonies, was applied both to individualism and business. In England application was generally restricted to only a few people compared to the way it was applied in the colonies. Whereas in England individualism and business were carried on by only a few, in the colonies it was virtually open to all. Today we would call it "economic opportunity." What is essential to the ultimate success of personal freedom is economic opportunity, which prospered in the colonies for a variety of reasons. For example, abundant resources in the form of land were available to anyone willing to work.

The case of Roger Williams is classic. He left New England and discovered a large piece of unused land between New England and New York. There he founded Rhode Island. This event illustrates a principle of the American economic system; namely, if you don't like where you are, you can leave with assurance that elsewhere there will be equal opportunity to make your fortune again. Today it works very little differently. For example, a man can be working for someone for ten to fifteen years and then decide to strike out on his own with very little resources, knowing full well he might fail. But at least he has had a chance. The assurance of second, third, and fourth chances at economic opportunity makes it possible for personal freedom to work.

All you need is to have a Russian immigrant describe the servile and whining attitude of the present-day Russian worker who early in life realizes that if he cannot successfully work where he is, he may very well never have an opportunity to work elsewhere. So he becomes a very slow worker. He continually tells the boss how right he is and seldom looks for new and different ways of doing things. Such a worker is, in effect, permanently dedicated to the idea of protecting the job he has. A worker who angers his superior will have difficulties equaling his present economic position elsewhere since his boss carries so much influence in what he may say about his former employee. To a lesser degree, perhaps, the same condition exists in much of Western Europe.

True, the principle of economic opportunity depends more on mental attitude than on resources. The engineer who quits the big company thinking he can redesign a product and become independent, perhaps a millionnaire, is motivated by his mental attitude.

Generally, colleges, universities, and the American educational system as a whole have done a terrible job in properly defining economic opportunity. Even chambers of commerce and other trade and professional associations comprised of businessmen make the mistake of talking about the necessity of profits to the American independent economic system. It is not profits that are essential—it is economic opportunity. And while economic opportunity may produce profits, it may also result in losses. More than seventy percent of all business operations in the United States either lose money or barely break even. The American realizes that when he shifts from one activity to another he may "lose his shirt." But he is exercising his prerogative of personal freedom.

The concept of economic opportunity as it has been practiced in the United States includes the realization that the entrepreneur, the businessman, the skilled employee, or whoever, can lose his money. The economics books do not say this. They use the term "risk," and there is a difference. One is a calculation; the other is a plain fact. It is true that American businessmen do not publicize their losses as they do their profits, but a cornerstone of the independent economic system in the United States is the "possibility of profit." It is not profit per se. If all you had to do to make a profit was to go into business for yourself, everybody would be there. It is the possibility of profits that dominates the psychology of economic opportunity and makes the business system work.

Nowhere was this more evident than in the thirteen colonies, where three million people pursued business every day in its traditional form of bargaining, negotiating, buying, and selling in a struggle for wealth by social cooperation and mutual exchange. They recognized that business was subject to rules and law. Throughout this period, as well as the next one hundred and fifty years of American history, much of the freedom of the entrepreneur, the businessman, or the self-employed was misused in an attempt by businessmen to take advantage of the customer, competitor, or his supplier through an unholy alliance with government. There were a host of such examples in the colonies at the time of the Revolution. "You cross my palm, I cross yours." "I support the Revolution, you buy your merchandise from me," etc. All of these, examples of the use of economic opportunity and personal freedom, merely reflect what was available to those people at that time.

No society ever had the opportunity to operate so freely in the same way. Freedom without economic opportunity is an empty word. So the concept of freedom did not exist under the primitive conditions of early man. Control was absolute and complete, usually supported by fear, taboos, and ties of blood, all aimed at self-preservation. When mankind moved into the periods of the slave states of Greece and Rome, control was absolute but subject to constant conflict. Again economic opportunity had little meaning. Property was held by the aristocrats and, even when owned by individuals, was often thought of as belonging to the state. In the Middle Ages when the church was dominant, society became largely static. Everybody had a specific status. A high percentage of the people remained in that status in exchange for their right to demand protection from the ruling lord.

It was, however, in the latter stages of the Middle Ages that free economy began, more or less under the supervision of the church. This period brought the first rudiments of commercialism as we know it today. During this period commercial activity grew into an easily controlled system called mercantilism. It was dominated by the ruling power, monarch, or church, and was based on hereditary rights through guilds of craftsmen who made it impossible for the individual to participate. It was against this system of organized tyranny, this mercantilism, that Adam Smith wrote his book claiming that free markets were a much better way to operate. Certainly, personal freedom was not consistent with mercantilism, which invariably involved import and export taxes as well as privileges to those who had seniority in training as contrasted to those who had just come to work to try to become specialists.

It was mercantilism that caused the British to pass a law that all foundry products had to be ordered from England and that the colonists could not open a foundry in Philadelphia. Through such laws the colonists could see that if they remained under British rule, these incidents, though few in number, were likely to occur more frequently.

It is true the colonists were fighting for personal freedom in their revolution, but they were also fighting for the continuation of their experience of one hundred and fifty years, that of maximizing economic opportunity. They judged that if they did not have the second they would never have voted for the first, so the two motivations went hand in hand.

Writing in the magazine, *The Public Interest,* on "The

9

Ethnic Miracle," Andrew M. Greeley points out that the United States gave the ethnic immigrants who came here between 1880 and 1920 "two things they would never have had in the old country: personal freedom and the opportunity to convert the hard work they took for granted into economic progress." In the old country, nothing was gained by hard work; in the United States there was at least the promise of a chance.

Greeley's article explains how the American dream was not limited just to those who came over in the early years either before the Revolutionary War or shortly thereafter. It is incredible that the Jews, the Irish Catholics, then the Italians and the Poles, in that order, immigrated to the United States where they were, in the majority of cases, hated, despised, and condemned to the point that attempts were made to bar their relatives from joining them. Nevertheless, by 1960 all four of these groups were able to demonstrate that they had produced higher family incomes than the overall American average and specifically higher than the national average for whites and the various other classifications of Protestants. They did it precisely as the Americans did in the years prior to the Revolution; namely through hard work, saving and sacrificing, and education. It is a great story and it is still going on today among minority groups, especially with the blacks since 1954 when they decided to become aggressive and seize their opportunities.

Today, we are out of touch with the thinking in earlier centuries. But for five thousand years the concept that the average citizen could govern himself was literally considered insane in most countries of the Western World. Birth and class had developed through the centuries as the all-important criteria. The concept that there was sufficient intelligence and ability at the lower levels of society for people to govern themselves was unbelievable. In North

America in the seventeenth and eighteenth centuries, upward mobility on a large scale became a reality for the first time.

The Declaration of Independence by-passed these centuries of absolutist opinion and in an imaginative way captured the hearts and minds of people, not only in the colonies, but throughout the world. In essence, the battle for the opinion of the masses was won by the Declaration of Independence. The only victory that remained to be won was that on the battlefield.

1

The Declaration of Independence

To set the stage for the Declaration of Independence one must understand not only the intangibles expressed above but also the developmental panorama of events that began in 1775 when war started in New England. Benjamin Franklin was the Machiavellian leader of the colonies, staying in the background, but advising, persuading, cajoling, and exerting never-ending pressure on the delegates to be more aggressive. John Adams was the bombastic spokesman and was frequently in the spotlight with his vitriolic attitude.

Much of the progress toward the Declaration of Independence coincided with the progress, or lack of it, of George Washington in the undeclared war. As he prepared to fight on Long Island, he implored Congress to take some action that would enable him to build morale among his troops—in other words, make a commitment as a nation so the troops would know what they were fighting for. Only thus would Washington have a better chance of getting more troops. This plea was used in a political way by the leaders of the independence movement in Congress to justify taking the aggressive step of actually declaring independence. Such a step had never before been taken in a precisely similar and exact manner as in the case of the colonies through their approval of the Declaration of Independence.

The declaration was approved by Congress on the morning of July 4 and the printing of it began that afternoon, continuing into the early morning hours of the fifth. Copies were sent throughout the colonies the following day and then many copies were reprinted locally. There is no doubt there was a tremendous groundswell of public opinion supporting the Declaration as it was proclaimed and that this voice of the public got back to Congress so that on July 19 they authorized the handwritten version. In effect, they had tested their product, sent it to the marketplace, got the reception, and decided to dramatize the incident—justifiably so.

The concept of something new and different must first be expressed before it can ever be achieved. This is true of products such as Xerox copiers, Polaroid cameras, or even the zipper. It is even more true of great ideas and great moments in the development of man, of which the greatest single moment overall is the expression contained in the Preamble of the Declaration of Independence. This was approved on July 2 and, of course, was the heart and soul of the document.

The ability of Congress to approve such a document without explaining its built-in conflicts, the most important being race, was another interesting exercise in mental gymnastics. It has frequently been treated, but never in a satisfactory manner, other than to say that the common

14

opinion of Congress was that everybody knew what was and was not included in the document. But this fundamental failure to deal with the problems of race and freedom at that time was to prove costly. It took a Civil War to resolve the conflict.

The story of the printed copy and its distribution throughout the colonies, and the subsequent use of a professional penman in preparing the written version, is virtually unknown. The handwritten copy was authorized on July 19, and signing by those present began on August 2 and continued for five years.

John Trumbull's painting contributed greatly to the misunderstanding that the signing was done at one time and place. However, the spirit of the Declaration of Independence that was present on July 4 was also there on August 2. The printed copy (whether it was signed by Hancock and Thomson is unknown) was in fact a dramatization of the formal approval that had taken place.

There were members of Congress present on July 4 who never had the opportunity to sign, and some members were present on August 2 who signed but who were not actually present and participating on July 4.

Twenty-one copies of the printed Declaration of Independence are known to exist. Only two are in private hands.

The Declaration of Independence as signed was a dramatic document. Its ringing words represented an emotional experience that appealed to all the patriots, and in a sense welded the colonies together. For one hundred and fifty years the Fourth of July was the single most celebrated holiday in the United States.

2

Richard Hooker
and
Natural Law

The roots of the Declaration of Independence are to be found deep in history. Not only are Aristotle and Cicero involved, but so are more modern thinkers such as St. Thomas Aquinas. For if these names are little more than just that, and the men's thoughts simply a part of the political amalgam of our time, their ideas are present in everyday American society.

But it was to the sixteenth century that men turned to discover more modern beginnings for the sort of society that was developing on the western shore of the Atlantic in the eighteenth century.

One of the most important of these was Richard Hooker, whose great accomplishment was to make Englishmen conscious of their heritage and the continuity of their history, which led inevitably to an expanding freedom at home. Hooker was born in Exeter in 1553 of

16

a distinguished, but not very wealthy family, and educated at Corpus Christi College of Oxford.

He soon became a tutor there and so well known at this occupation that Edwin Sandys, Bishop of London, insisted that his son Edwin be sent to Corpus Christi to study under Hooker, who was then nineteen years old. (That study would bear fruit in America, as will be shown in the chapter on the Virginia charter.)

It was Hooker's fortune to live in the days of Queen Elizabeth at a time when she was puzzling over the proper relationship between the crown and the church, or as we would put it today, state and church.

The Church of Rome had become a monarchical institution. But in England, feudalism was gone, and from that came the idea that although the Pope was head of the Papal State, he was not entitled to any more political rights than any other king.

Hooker's argument was purely ecclesiastical in its setting and was occasioned in his last years, when he wrote extensively on the relations of the church and society, by the growth of the Puritan religion.

What he attempted to do was to find a justification in reason as well as faith for the establishment—the Church of England as an official part of the governing apparatus of the nation.

And so, in his later years, as the sixteenth century drew to an end, he worked to this purpose, producing at least five works that came to be known as The Laws of Ecclesiastical Policy.

This matter became increasingly important in English society when Elizabeth died and James became king.

Essentially, and in a modern European form, Hooker restated the concept of Aristotle, that the purpose of society is not to enable men to live, but to live well. By this he meant the guidance of religion, but one can see the extensions of the philosophy, even so.

Hooker's societies could be classified into three groups: those where church and society were distinct bodies. These he called infidel. The second group was the Catholic society where church and society were one, but the sovereignty was divided between pope and emperor. Third was Anglican society, where church and society were one body, undivided.

Hooker's treatises, of course, were an attempt to find rationale for the odd religious situation of England after the departure from the realm of Rome. Nonetheless, they established certain principles that were widely accepted at the time as well as in later years.

One principle involves the place of king and society: that no one part of society has power to exercise authority, that the king has to maintain divine law, not make it, and that law is superior to the king. Therefore, said Hooker, the highest authority in England in civil affairs was Parliament, and in religion, the Convocation.

From this came the idea that the state derives its authority from the will of the people and the consent of the governed.

In this sense, then, the Reformation and its rationale provided a stepping-stone toward a freer England than had existed before.

In his day, Hooker had not the slightest conception that a state could be considered as a purely secular institution. His whole argument was based on religious grounds, although he conceived of government as having a material as well as a moral function. Thus the organ of government must be prepared to deal with both moral and material problems.

So in **Hooker** there can be seen the point of change in Western society. He is the last of the medievals in that sense, the last important philosopher to consider natural law in the medieval fashion. The difference was that Hooker and those before him considered mankind in relation to God. The medieval philosophers believed that man was made in the image of God, that human nature contained a divine element, and that all human success was caused by divine will. Thus church and state could and should be inseparable.

But even as he emphasized this position, Hooker set up the floors and opened the doors for another sort of consideration of government. Remove the churchly aspects of Hooker's program and there exists the king as head of state, who rules with the consent of the people, which is expressed through Parliament.

In the years after Hooker, this idea began to gather strength, and when in the seventeenth century it was thrown upon new virgin shores, where men had to create their own society out of the wilderness, the authority of church moved farther away while that of the material government became paramount.

Hooker had planted thoughts that would mature both in England and in America in the next one hundred and fifty years.

3

The Virginia Assembly

Considering the political events that culminated in the Declaration of Independence, *idea* was a vital factor, and for this the pages must be turned back to Aristotle and the Republic of Athens.

In that sense, the line of progression is that of Western European society, and yet some things happened in the period that began with the colonization by Europe of outward areas that were to be equally important and more germane to the specific development of the North American colonies.

At the beginning of the seventeenth century, England had not a single colony in Asia, Africa, or the Americas. By the end of the century she had some twenty flourishing colonies in the Americas. For the first time Englishmen were going abroad to live for long periods, perhaps forever, in a manner that indicated soon enough that some different ideas must be offered in methods of government.

When the Virginia colony was settled, its business and government affairs were in the hands of the Virginia Company of Plymouth, for local administration, and the Virginia Company of London, which was responsible to the Crown.

The Virginia Company of the new world, and particularly Sir Edwin Sandys, had a broad dream of the future. Sandys and others tried to obtain a new charter for Virginia to give them more latitude. They failed. They tried to secure a new tobacco contract with the mother country. In this they failed as well. They also tried to establish a new method of supplying the colony with all that was needed, including people. This program failed and eventually brought about the bankruptcy of the company.

But the Virginia Company was to leave one permanent political legacy that would affect life on the American continent. It was to be the *Charter of Grants and Liberties,* and eventually it would be attacked at home as a dreadful example of "popularness" and "democratical" experiment.

Sometime during the summer of 1618, Sir Edwin counseled with several of his peers in Virginia. He was far more interested in the government of the colony than in trade, although he was assistant treasurer. Sir Thomas Smith, treasurer, and Alderman Robert Johnson, sometime sheriff, were other powers in the government, but their interest was more largely commercial. And thus Sir Edwin, by trading off commercial for political power, had his way.

The charter was a long and detailed document, dealing with the privileges, orders, and laws to govern the colony. It outlined the method of making land grants providing that the company would retain these grants instead of delegating them to the resident governor. It gave rules for the location of new plantations and stipulated quitrents and taxes.

But more important, it presented a body of laws to govern the colony and stated some underlying principles of government, such as that of "a free state in Virginia" and no government to be imposed on the colonists except by their own consent.

This idea had developed over the past score of years in the pulling and hauling of the colonists against the mother country. The longer the colonists stayed, the more they saw that they and not London knew how to deal with local conditions. And when London's statements and demands sometimes proved impossible, sometimes simply ludicrous, the feeling grew that London should mind its own business.

One important factor was the establishment of the right to vote. The age was set at seventeen, and voting referred to "inhabitants," which meant freeholders (land), householders, free servants, and *indentured servants*. Since there were no blacks in the colony, that question did not arise. Women and children, of course, were not considered as voters.

Late in the Summer of 1618, Sir Edwin's charter was ready for discussion. Elections were held in the various communities after June 19 and on July 30, 1619, there assembled in the choir of the Church at Jamestown what would go down as the first legislative body ever to meet in America.

John Pory was selected as Speaker. He sat in front of Governor Sir George Yeardley, and the clerk, John Twine, sat next to the councillors, who were ranged on either side of the room. They were twenty-two in all.

The group listened to a prayer for their good work by

the Reverend Mr. Buck, took the oath, and then settled down to business.

This assembly of 1619 lasted six days. They could hardly have chosen a worse time for it; the weather was infuriatingly hot, and the speaker soon came down with some rheum—probably malaria. So bad were the conditions that one member of the assembly died during the proceedings and many of the others were ill.

At the end of that time, admitting that they had been hasty because of the intemperate weather, the group broke up. But they had enacted Sir Edwin's basic law, and for five years they would live under it.

The assembly met again the following March and then several times again in the months and years that ensued. Meanwhile, the affairs were going badly in a business sense, and that is what counted with the financiers in England who had backed the venture. They cared little for the manner of government, as long as it did not threaten to become too "democratick" and as long as the colony was profitable. But bad weather, Indian troubles, and finally a dreadful massacre destroyed the economy of Virginia.

Many other changes had come about as well. By 1624 a new governor had come to the colony and the makeup of the assembly was almost entirely different from that of 1619.

In its last meeting in February and March 1624, the assembly spent much of its time composing petitions to the king and Privy Council; already from London had come rumors that the company was about to be dissolved because of its bad performance.

The assembly made two requests. It begged the Privy Council to recognize the right of the local council to act in an advisory capacity to the governor. It also asked that no taxes be imposed on the colonists without the consent of the General Assembly.

In London these requests were ignored. King and council had the feeling that the Virginians had over-reached themselves, become far too "popular" and "democratick."

Then King James died and King Charles took the throne, and many a change was made in the administration of England itself. But the changes that affected Virginia were for the most part repressive. The colony was taken over by the king, and from that time until 1638 no certain decision as to the form of government for Virginia was really reached.

That year, in spite of appeals from Sir Edwin and others, a special commission in London recommended that a new Virginia company be established, but one that reserved to the king, "the supreme and royal power of the government."

Even so, the Assembly of 1619 had accomplished a major change in the society of North America. Under the royal patent, the House of Burgesses was regularly assembled and enjoined to make laws "correspondent as near as may be to the laws of England"; but of course the royal governor was to have the power of veto.

Forever more the 1619 meeting had established a precedent: the people of a royal colony were to have a share in the making of the laws, the levying of taxes. They were, in effect, to be partly self-governing. It was a vital change. Its first application had failed, but the idea would live.

4

Roger Williams and the Founding
of Rhode Island

Americans revere the Pilgrim fathers and the Puritan ancestors who settled in Massachusetts, but not because they contributed very much positively to the general idea of freedom. In their dissent—their own demand to be free and untrammeled in the pursuit of their religion and their way of life—they soon enough became oppressors of all who believed differently.

Nor were most of the leaders democratic or anything like it in the concept of mankind. If they offered any suggestion at all in this regard, it may have been their practice of choosing governors by the whole body of those qualified persons.

But in a negative way the Puritans of New England did contribute to the development of political thought in America. They made life so miserable for dissenters that many of them fled beyond Puritan boundaries. Principal among these was an offender against religious laws, Roger Williams.

For his "crimes," Williams was banished from Massachusetts Bay Colony on October 9, 1635. It was the intent of the authorities at Boston to send him back to England on a ship that was just getting ready to sail, and they dispatched an officer to Salem to apprehend Williams and to see that he got on the ship.

But Williams was warned, and three days before his pursuer arrived, he was gone, heading south toward Narragansett. He chose this place because it was a gap in the English colonies—neither the crown nor any others had made patents or claims on this land. He traveled through the wilderness with a companion and took refuge with the Indians, staying with them in their "filthy smoke holes" for nearly fourteen weeks in the worst of the winter.

He bought land from the great chief Massasoit near the Seekonk River. Soon he was joined by other exiles, and after some negotiating they settled on the eastern bank of Narragansett Bay at the juncture of the Moshassuc and the Wanasquatucket. The government they established was the simplest possible form, sufficient to manage the affairs of a very small community. The heads of families and the young men of age met once a fortnight to discuss problems and settle them by agreement. They signed a compact to subject themselves to the will of the majority "until they should hear further the King's pleasure"—*but only "in civil things."*

Thus was laid a root of religious tolerance.

Five years after his banishment, Williams began writing some of his ideas. His first major work was "The Bloudy Tenent"—a reference to the persecution of the Puritans.

Williams viewed the church not as a part of government or the government as the Puritans would have it, but as one of a group of different bodies that the state was bound to protect.

He clearly separated church and state and espoused the radical theory of liberty of conscience. In matters religious, the church authorities were to have complete control, but they were not to interfere in nonreligious matters.

Williams also expressed some extremely radical ideas for his day, one being the concept that there were admirable persons in the world who did not believe as he did and who might not even be Christians. And so he invited "Papists, Protestants, Jews and Turks" to come and live with him. In other words, here for the first time was the concept of absolute religious equality, including the right not to believe in anything.

Roger Williams contributed several other major efforts to the body politic on the North American shore.

Very quickly Williams realized that if Rhode Island were to remain intact and proof against the ambitions of the surrounding colonies, there must be mutual cooperation among the towns that were springing up. In 1643 Massachusetts and Plymouth were pressing claims, and he decided to go to England.

He was forbidden by Massachusetts authorities to come to Boston, even to sail from there, so he went to the Dutch colony of New Amsterdam and sailed to England. There he secured the patent to the colony that protected Rhode Island from incursions. In May 1647 a group of free men met at Portsmouth to organize a government and draw up a body of laws. They created a federal system in which the individual towns became a part of the larger community, the colony. It was the first centralization of control in this manner.

The system and the laws established were one of the earliest made for any body of men in America and the first to bring in all the precedents set by the laws of England.

The government was to be "democratical." The federal, or central, government consisted of a president, four assistants, a recorder, a treasurer, and a sergeant. These men were to be nominated by the towns and chosen by "the court of election" in May, the court consisting of representatives from each town.

To keep the central government from being too powerful, certain safeguards were begun. They included frequent elections, the right of the towns to initiate legislation, the recall privilege by which towns could ask for popular vote on undesirable laws, and the referendum by which the legislators could refer laws to the people before enactment.

Rhode Island's government also brought other ideas into being in the next few years. It was the first colony to adopt a bill of rights, simple, in four general provisions. This was a forerunner to the Bill of Rights of the United States Constitution.

Not all these developments survived long. Williams was hampered because he was not a lawyer and had no training in matters of statesmanship, so many of his ideas did not last long; they ran against the temper of the times.

He envisioned the right of all men to have a part in the government, but this was quickly abrogated by defining a free man as a landowner and not as an individual.

Even the liberty of soul was curtailed. In 1729 the Catholics were disfranchised in Rhode Island.

His idea that all forms of government should rest on popular consent was diminished over the years—by the landowners in particular.

And thus came the common statement in the colonies in later days that Rhode Island differed from Massachusetts because Massachusetts had law but not liberty, and Rhode Island had liberty but not law.

It was a lesson that would not be forgotten in the loom of history: liberty could exist only under law.

5

Thomas Hooker's Connecticut

On July 7, 1635, a group of men in London authorized John Winthrop, Jr. to go to New England and, at the mouth of the Connecticut River, to lay out lands, build a fort, and erect houses suitable for himself and "other men of quality."

Winthrop came, and very soon the Reverend Thomas Hooker of Massachusetts decided he would leave the colony where he was as dissatisfied with restrictions as Roger Williams had been (though he was not so much in disfavor). So the following year Hooker and a number of his followers moved to Connecticut.

Hooker was no Williams. Indeed, had he been accused of such free thinking he would have been insulted. Still he fretted under the strictures of Puritanism, and as an intelligent man, he had some definite ideas as to how a colony should be run. Principal among these was the concept he shared and discussed with several others, that authority should be vested in the part of the people deemed competent to exercise it.

Although he disagreed with Williams, Hooker arrived at the same general concept of freedom by a different route, and the first government of Connecticut reflected this view.

That government was a commission, established March 3, 1636. Eight men were to have full power and authority to exercise judicial functions, to make orders and decrees, to regulate trade and planting, and to call the inhabitants together at any time to carry out their instructions. It was in this manner that the basis for popular government was assured.

That government lasted only one year, but its importance lies in the fact that it was not imposed from above but represented the free will of those inhabitants of Connecticut.

For two years the area was governed under simple laws. Then, meeting to work out a better form, the leaders of the community heard on May 31, 1638, the Reverend Hooker's sermon, which he devoted to the concept of government and the people.

The foundations of all authority, said Hooker, were laid in the free consent of "the people." What was different here was Hooker's concept of "the people," for it was much broader than any that had been expressed earlier by others.

Even then the Connecticut idea was a long way from the sort of democracy we think of in the twentieth century. Its concern was basically the community and not the individual.

6

The Virginia Charter

The Virginia colony had its ups and downs in the seventeenth century, but it continued to grow under the Cromwellian government. But when Charles II was restored to the throne in 1660, the fortunes of Virginia suddenly received a setback.

The colony was made to realize the power of the king, Parliament, and certain absentee lords who had great influence in Virginia.

The first really obnoxious occurrence was the decision of Parliament in 1660 to bring all colonial tobacco to England for market. Since the warehouses of London were already bulging with tobacco, the price to the growers kept going down.

High taxes, hard times, and invasion by the Dutch all brought unhappiness to the colonists in Virginia, but one act by King Charles in 1673 shocked them more than all others.

Back in 1649 the exiled Charles had granted to a number of his royal followers all of the territory called the Northern Neck, which runs between the Rappahannock and Potomac rivers. Of course, as long as he was king-in-exile, these grants meant nothing; they were a way of rewarding his followers and securing their financial support.

The gamble paid off when he was restored, and suddenly the grants became real.

Later, in 1673, the king gave to Lords Arlington and Thomas Culpepper the remaining part of Virginia to the south. Thus, by the stroke of a pen, huge tracts of land, planted in tobacco and other crops, improved by the settlers who lived in the area, suddenly passed into the ownership of a handful of British lords.

Who were they, mused the colonists about themselves, slaves whose lands and work were to be tossed about like chaff in a wind?

In the Fall of 1674, a group of thoroughly disgruntled men met at Jamestown to consider ways in which they might protect themselves from this high-handed treatment.

The plan on which they agreed was to send three agents to London to plead with the king and arrange to buy out these proprietors. Further, they were to establish the rights of Virginians in the new land.

They also had with them the draft of a charter that they hoped would secure these rights.

The charter gave the local assembly considerable power. It granted to the Virginians the right to their lands forever. It gave the power of trial, punishment, and mercy to the governors and council, except in matters of treason and murder, which were reserved for the crown. Furthermore, it gave to the assembly the supreme power to make laws for Virginians subject only to review by the crown.

And, except for duty on goods sent to London, the governor, the council, and the burgesses would have the sole power of levying taxes in the colony.

Here, in 1674, was a clear indication of how the people of the colonies were beginning to feel about the imposition of authority from above. It was less than a century since they had come to the new world. They had enjoyed freedoms here that had not existed for them in the old world, the greatest of them being the freedom of movement in an open, unsettled land. To many this was worth all the hardship that accompanied their life in America.

In the earlier years, and in the turmoil of the Cromwell years, America had been left fairly well alone. But with the restoration of the monarchy under Charles II, more attention was being paid to what was happening on the western shores of the Atlantic, and the colonists did not like it.

The charter, had it been enacted, could very well have started the colonies off on a new direction that would have precluded future troubles.

It did secure serious consideration in London. It was taken as far as the Privy Council, where it died—some said by the action, very privately taken, of the king himself.

Any thought of reconsidering it vanished in Bacon's Rebellion, which history records as an uprising of hardworking colonists who objected to taxation that deprived them of the fruit of their labor.

Nathaniel Bacon was born in 1647 in Suffolk, England. He was the son of a well-to-do upper-class family, and his prospects were bright. But when he married, he incurred the enmity of his father-in-law, a noble who quickly disinherited his daughter.

To better his fortunes, Bacon became involved in a scheme to defraud an acquaintance of his inheritance, and was in danger of going to prison, if not the Tower. So he found it wise to migrate to the new world.

There he sought Virginia, because Sir William Berkeley, the royal governor, was his cousin by marriage. Bacon quickly acquired two large estates on the James River, and being then so affluent and important a citizen, was appointed to the governor's council.

Soon enough he quarreled with the governor. The immediate reason was Indian policy. The governor was trying to get along with the Indians in the West, but Bacon wanted to pursue a resolutely expansionist plan. So he organized a force and set out after the Indians in 1676.

The governor declared him to be in rebellion, and the struggle was on in earnest.

Bacon had it all his own way. Within a matter of months he won control of most of Virginia. And then, at the height of success, fighting against colonial policy laid down at home, Nathaniel Bacon died, and his rebellion collapsed.

In London the rebellion had emphasized more than ever to the crown the necessity for keeping the American colonies under a tight rein. "The rebellion of Virginia," said the Privy Council, "was occasioned by the excessive power of the Assembly."

The Virginians did obtain a charter in 1676, but it was far from what they wanted. The king confirmed the right to hold property, but he did not confirm the guarantee of all the rights of Englishmen, and particularly the right of acceptance before they were taxed.

A hundred years would go by, but Virginians would not forget.

7

Unrest in Maryland

Many years after the signing of the Declaration of Independence, a newspaper editor in the Far West would sit down one day to compose a slogan for his publication.

"There is no hope for the satisfied man," he would write.

Such definition certainly fit the colonists of Maryland in the last third of the seventeenth century.

Maryland was a proprietary colony, which meant that the proprietor, Lord Baltimore, had been granted such rights as made the whole area one big estate. Of course, he began selling it off for money, and the colonists, who had no recourse, accepted the state of affairs that existed.

But by 1676, when the reverberations of Bacon's rebellion in Virginia were seeping across the Potomac, they had welcome listeners in the dissatisfied colonists of Maryland.

All the elements were there: high taxes, arbitrary government by a proprietor and his governors, and Indian troubles.

And some men decided on action. They gathered in Calvert County, north of St. Mary's between Chesapeake Bay and the Patuxent River, one day in August, 1676. There were about sixty of them; excited men on horses, carrying rifles and pistols and even swords, and all heading for Thomas Barbary's plantation.

At the head of the column rode two men, Williams Davyes and John Pate, both respectable farmers who had suddenly been caught up in the revolutionary fervor. They had with them a paper listing grievances and insisted that it be considered by the highest authorities.

The messengers of the governor's council met them and listened—and then arbitrarily told them to go home. All would be pardoned except the leaders, they said ominously.

Davyes and Pate then called their men and the sixty wheeled about and rode away to the beat of their own drums.

That was as far as it went. The governor's soldiers were soon on the march and they chased Davyes and Pate to New Castle on the Delaware, where they caught them and took them back to "the Clifts" of Calvert County. Here the two leaders of a rebellion that had never gotten started were hanged on the banks of the Chesapeake.

The event served the ostensible purpose of intimidating the Marylanders.

Why were Davyes and Pate hanged? Their bill of grievances shows the situation:

They objected to high taxes. Every man had to pay 297 pounds of tobacco each year. The poor man with little land or poor land paid as much as the rich. A free man who had no estate still paid the taxes but could not vote for representatives to the council.

That was the extent of their complaint.

The governor and the council then lectured the people. Davyes and Pate had been hanged, they said, not because they brought grievances, ill-considered as those were. They had been hanged because the law must be upheld, and it was against the law to bring grievances before the council's representatives by force. In other words, there would be no change.

And so, in 1676, in Maryland an anonymous document suddenly came into being; for obvious reasons it was unsigned—Marylanders now knew the penalties of dissent.

It was called "The Complaint from Heaven," and it was written in a style to suggest some unlettered backwoodsman. But the arguments and ideas presented were anything but those of unlettered men.

"Complaint from Heaven" was a biting attack on the proprietary system and Lord Baltimore and his government.

It accused Baltimore of high crimes and misdemeanors against the crown and against the people. It declared that he had made himself a "prince" in Maryland, and, in essence, it called for the king to seize Maryland, make it a royal colony, and grant certain rights to the colonists.

The rights included universal suffrage for free men and establishment of a legislative branch of government that would have real power.

Within the framework of the existing English government and loyalty to the crown, the Marylanders of 1676 were talking as revolutionaries.

8

The Charter of Libertyes

In 1664 when the Dutch were forced out of Nieuw Amsterdam and the British undertook the rule of the colony that had been New Holland, King Charles gave the colony to his younger brother, James, Duke of York. Thus, New York was named.

To manage his affairs, the duke, of course, sent a governor, a person he regarded as a sort of supernumerary or keeper of estate, but one who had enormous power over the lives of the inhabitants.

For example, without much thought, the duke gave away New Jersey to the proprietors Berkeley and Carteret. He gave Delaware County to William Penn. The people who lived in these places had no say at all about it.

New York had no local legislative body. The Dutch had never had one, for their colony was originally organized as part of a trading company. The Stuart kings were not much in favor of elected legislatures, and so the body of law was simply laid down by the governor in the duke's name and called The Duke's Laws.

In the war of 1672 the Dutch captured New York again and held it until the signing of the Treaty of Westminster two years later. By this time the colonists were becoming more strident in discussing the need for a local legislative body.

The new governor, Major Edmund Andros, suggested to the duke that he might make more profit from the colony if he allowed the colonists to have the feeling that they shared in their own taxation.

The duke thought it a dreadful idea. It was, he said, simply an imitation of the other colonies in North America and he wanted no part of it.

By 1680 the New Yorkers still did not have any sort of an assembly.

Resentment mounted steadily, and that year the merchants and businessmen had a chance to show their feelings. The duke had posted a list of customs rates on trade, which ran from 1677 to 1680. The rates were for three-year periods so that the duke would have the option of raising them every three years.

The rates expired at a time when Governor Andros was off in London explaining why he was not making as much money from the colony as the duke thought he should be.

When the rates expired, the merchants refused to pay any more duties. Customs Collector William Dyer cajoled them. It did not do any good. He brought soldiers to make his collections. Those who were forced paid, but they began talking about the Magna Carta, the Petition of Right, and other English statutes, and accused Dyer of subverting the laws of England and of treason to the crown.

Such talk was very unsettling. A grand jury was called and charged him with these high crimes. The court, afraid of the duke, did not want anything to do with the case and packed the collector off to England where he received a promotion.

But the whole affair started people talking in the coffee houses of Manhattan that such indecencies would not occur if they only had a local assembly that could put laws to rights when needed. And they managed to get the point across to the duke that he was losing money and would lose more unless the people got their legislature.

And so, with great reluctance, the duke was convinced that he must give in if he wanted to continue to profit from the colony.

Thus in August, 1683, Colonel Thomas Dongan, the new governor who would replace Andros, arrived with instructions to let the people have their legislature.

On October 17, 1683, the first assembly met at Fort James. It consisted of eighteen members, all elected in one way or another, some by free men, some by appointed freeholders. These men set about creating the Charter of Libertyes and Priviledges.

The legislative authority of the colony, under the king and the duke, was to reside in a governor, council, and the people meeting in a General Assembly. And they were to have *all* power to make the laws.

This charter guaranteed the right of freeholders and free men to vote, and defined them under the laws of England. It guaranteed the liberty of person, the right of property, trial by jury, no excessive bail, and guarantees against quartering troops in private houses in peacetime.

The framers of the charter devoted a good deal of attention to the rights and responsibilities of the legislature, including the protection of its members by such devices as the provision that the legislature was to be the sole arbiter of the qualifications of its members. This would prevent undue interference from the governor or the duke. Also, assembly members were to be free from arrest while going to and from the legislature.

One long section of this charter was devoted to religion because New York, for its time, had a remarkably mixed population of Puritans and Dutch Protestants, Catholics, Quakers, and all the rest. Freedom of religion was guaranteed.

The power to tax, above all, was placed in the hands of the new legislature. And the lower house, the freeholders' direct representatives, was given the sole power to originate money bills. That certainly put power in the hands of the people.

The problem then was to get the charter past the governor and then the duke.

The governor was easily maneuvered into position. One of the first laws passed by the new legislature provided that Governor Dongan should have a penny on the pound of value of all real and personal property belonging to freeholders and free men.

How could Dongan refuse? Only a crazy man would turn down a fortune offered him on a platter. He went along.

And so on October 31, 1683, with the sound of trumpets in City Hall, the charter was promulgated and published as an established fact.

And then the charter went to England.

The duke's advisers at court seemed to accept the idea and the duke was persuaded that this system would, indeed, bring him in a greater return from his far-off American colony. So he signed the charter, sealed it, and sent it to the auditor to dispatch it officially to New York.

Then something happened that nobody could have anticipated. Charles II died and James, Duke of York, became James II, King of England.

Suddenly, it no longer seemed important that he have those revenues from New York. It was far more important that the American colonies be brought under control.

And so the Charter of Libertyes, the dream, was turned to dross.

9

John Locke's Treatises
of Government

The famous political philosopher John Locke is connected with the American colonies in several ways.

For one, he was involved in the writing of the first charter and constitution of the South Carolina colony.

In 1663, a number of courtiers at Charles II's court maneuvered the king into giving them land in the Americas. Principal among these was Sir Anthony Ashley Cooper, later Anthony, Lord Ashley, and still later the Earl of Shaftesbury.

Shaftesbury was constantly interested in the colonies and had a hand in the framing of the government of Maryland, among others. He had first been deeply interested in Barbados and had invested heavily there.

Shaftesbury and seven others secured from the king in 1663 the lands lying between the 36th and 31st degrees of northern latitude, and extending westward "to the south seas," which meant as far as anyone knew. They held territory that extended from Virginia south to the Florida line, a huge block of wilderness.

They tried to colonize the area, made maps, and sent people to Cape Fear. The colony failed.

They managed to persuade some Virginians to come south into the shore of Albemarle Sound, and from this came the province of Albemarle, which would later be North Carolina. Charles Town (Charleston) was settled but the area just seemed unable to attract colonists.

In 1666 Shaftesbury became the patron of educator John Locke and secured his help in trying to save the colony. Locke wrote an appeal to persuade the people not to leave Cape Fear as they were doing. It failed. They then planned three new towns, and the proprietors sent three ships with colonists to the area.

In 1668 Locke became Secretary to the Lords Proprietors of Carolina and helped draft the constitution for that government. (A copy of that constitution in Locke's hand is in the Public Records Office in London, but how much he had to do with its essentials is debatable.)

The *Fundamental Constitutions for the Government of Carolina* were drawn to avoid the sort of democracy that was sweeping across the American colonies and to establish firmly the position of the "lords proprietors."

For his work, Locke was created a "Landgrave in the Aristocracy of Carolina," a title he and his heirs were to hold forever. He also was given four thousand "baronia," or "estates," of land.

The political framework of the colony was to be a manorial system. It was to have two legislative bodies, a people's assembly, and an assembly of the aristocracy, and the constitution was weighted so that the aristocracy could control.

There would be religious toleration, but belief in God was compulsory. "No man shall be permitted to be a free man of Carolina, or have any estate of habitation in it who does not acknowledge a God and that God is publicly to be worshipped."

As it turned out, the Fundamental Constitutions never came into effect in Carolina. The proprietors lost favor at court, the whole kingdom changed, and the supremacy of the Lords Proprietors was repudiated even as people were beginning to settle the area.

So Locke's aristocratic title, and his barony in the new world, never came to anything; and his labors on the constitution came to nothing, nor would this adventure, if widely promulgated, have added to his reputation.

To a very great extent, the burning issue in England's political life of this period of the seventeenth century involved religion: the quarrel and struggle between the Roman Catholics and the church founded in the time of Henry VIII. This struggle involved machinations in France, Spain, and Rome. And in this conflict Locke was deeply involved as a determined Protestant. Late in 1675, Locke went to France and there he discovered that Protestants had a good deal better position than they had in England.

Locke was then forty-three years old, at the height of his vigor, and he learned much about the political affairs of the European continent.

He was back in England in 1678 and there found the fortunes of the Protestants much improved and those of the Catholics much worsened. That fall King Charles' feelings about the Catholics underwent considerable change when the Earl of Shaftesbury, leader of the Protestant cause, discovered a charge that there was a Catholic plot to kill the king, which became known as the Popish Plot.

Whether the plot was real or a trumped-up matter involving a known scoundrel named Titus Oates was immaterial. England suddenly became fearful of "Jesuit atrocities," and a number of Catholics who were arrested and tortured confessed to all manner of wrongdoing. The Catholics of the realm were disgraced. Some went into hiding and nearly all feared for their freedom, if not their lives.

And Lord Shaftesbury, leader of the zealot Protestants, secured the power in Parliament he wanted. Soon he, who had been in the Tower not long before, was Lord President of the King's Council.

But Charles, who disliked and distrusted Parliament, and particularly Shaftesbury, soon had dismissed Parliament. Shaftesbury was arrested once again.

Locke and Shaftesbury were friends, and Locke respected the politician because he was patriotic and a lover of freedom.

Now began in England a literary debate. Sir Robert Filmer published a book called *Patriarcha,* which was in effect an espousal of the principle of absolute monarchy.

This roused a number of others to reply. Among them was Locke who, in 1681, wrote *Two Treatises of Government.* Rather, he began writing them, for he revised them several times over the next few years. But they were conceived in the heat of the important argument made public during the reign of a very strong-willed king.

Locke attacked Filmer's contention that because men were born into subjection to their parents, they were therefore born into political subjection. And, he said, princes were no more than theoretical fathers of their people. Nor could there be any "divine right" of monarchy; no man could base a title to rule another on his descent from Adam, all knowledge of the line having been long lost.

47

In the Second Treatise, Locke considered the question of the origins of power. He rejected the cynical position that all power is the product only of force and violence. And he brought up an idea that was not new—the thought that civil government originated in a social contract.

He offered the theory that men had once lived in "a state of nature," which was nothing more or less than anarchy, and that they had agreed to come together and devise governments for the promotion of their common interests.

Locke said that liberty was one of the natural rights men brought with them from the state of nature into civil society. And by creating political societies they actually increased their liberty.

Locke also held some revolutionary views on the matter of property and ownership. Property, he believed, was a natural right, because property was created by man's own labor. One of the chief ends of society must be the preservation of property.

And then he said:

"The end of civil society is to avoid and remedy those inconveniences of the state of nature which necessarily follow from every man's being judge of his own case, by setting up a known authority to which everyone of that society may appeal upon any injury received or controversy that may arise and which everyone of the society ought to obey. . . ."

In other words, another major end of society was the provision of a system of justice.

Government, according to Locke, had the duty only to preserve the life, liberty, and property of the governed. And "when any number of men have so consented to make one common unity or government, they are thereby presently incorporated and made one body politic, wherein the majority have a right to act and conclude the rest. . . ."

In other words, the people had the right to decide on the form of government under which they would live. And in this Locke used the word "consented," for consent of the people was, in his view, the sole basis of public authority.

Locke also considered the question of rebellion and rulership. Since the exercise of civil power was a trust placed in the hands of the rulers by the people, then, said Locke, if a ruler violated the trust, the citizens would not only be morally justified in removing him but it was their moral duty to do so.

The last chapter of this second Treatise was entitled, "Of the Dissolution of Government."

"Wherever law ends, tyranny begins, if the law be transgressed to another's harm. And whosoever in authority exceeds the power given him by the law, and makes use of the force he has under his command to compass that upon the subject which the law allows not, ceases . . . to be a magistrate, and acting without authority may be opposed as any other man who by force invades the rights of another."

Thus revolution was justified. The sovereign who used unjustified force created a situation in which it was lawful to resist him.

If in a monarchy the prince set up his own arbitrary will in place of the laws, then he was changing the legislative function. If he hindered the legislative body from meeting, he was again altering the situation. If he interfered with the manner of election of the legislative body, he was interfering with basic rights, and in so doing, the prince in actuality dissolved the government, and the people had a right to replace it with another.

For if a ruler tried to take away or destroy the property of the people or to reduce them to slavery, the ruler put himself into a state of war with the people and absolved them of any further responsibility for obedience. The obvious next step was rebellion.

Soon enough Locke was in trouble, partly because of his ideas, partly because of his associations with Shaftesbury and the Protestant leaders. He fled to Holland where he remained for several years as the English constitutional and religious crisis deepened and finally culminated in "the glorious revolution" of 1688. He returned in the reign of William and Mary, was well received, and took his place as a leading intellectual figure in England.

In the ensuing years, one of his major contributions to English society was his struggle to secure an end to the Act for the Regulation of Printing by which the crown controlled the press. And, by arguing in favor of free trade in this matter, he achieved what other idealists had failed to do; he secured the abolition of this noxious law and the establishment of the principle of freedom of the press in England. "I know not why a man should not have liberty to print whatever he would speak and to be answerable for the one just as he is for the other. . . ."

Locke's writing, of course, covered far more than revolutionary political theory. He wrote much on education and his "Essay Concerning Human Understanding" is perhaps his most famous work. In later life he was appointed a Commissioner for Trade by the crown and he served in that capacity for several years, writing, engaging in intellectual controversies of the time, and offering ideas to a welcoming public.

Locke died in the fall of 1704. In his last years he was far more concerned with his studies of human understanding and human nature than he was with government. But as far as America was concerned, his *Treatises on Government* would become by far the most important words he ever wrote.

10

The Glorious Revolution

When Prince William landed on the shores of Tor Bay in southwestern England on November 5, 1688, and James II fled the royal court, a new era in the history of the rights of Englishmen began.

James had been an arbitrary and capricious ruler, and the rights of colonists in America had suffered badly from his whims. Colonial charters had been revoked, colonial privileges denied, and the new world was very much in turmoil when the coming of William brought welcome change.

The rights of Englishmen were reaffirmed and secure at home. Parliament, which had been dissolved by James and had not met for more than three years, suddenly reappeared, Whiggish in nature—which meant in those days almost revolutionary—and won for itself a much larger role in governing England.

But, coming into power, it took Parliament hardly a year to become far more conservative in outlook, particularly in matters concerning the overseas colonies.

In Boston the governor, Sir Edmund Andros, had cut a destructive swath through the colony's liberties, especially in the matter of religion, for James, of course, was a Roman Catholic.

Then during the first week of April, 1689, a traveler named John Winslow reached Boston from Nevis in the West Indies with a copy of Prince William's declaration from The Hague that he was moving to save England.

Winslow was clapped in jail by the governor's men, charged with holding "seditious and treasonable papers." He was soon out and so was the secret.

On April 18, hundreds of Boston men took up arms and marched down to the harbor. To the beat of drums they moved along. Something was in the air. What that was soon became clear. When Captain John George of His Majesty's frigate *Rose* came ashore, he was seized by the mob and held hostage against the possible use of the frigate's guns to attack the town. Boston was in open rebellion against the crown!

A group of the more prominent citizens met at the Town House and demanded the presence of Governor Andros. He was safe in the fort but he came out to talk, whereupon he was seized and jailed, along with some twenty of his leading adherents among the colonists.

One of the leaders of this crowd was Cotton Mather, son of Increase Mather, the agent for the colony in recent negotiations with London. The Reverend Mather and several other men of the cloth were as quick as any to move that day.

From Charlestown and other communities nearby, men began pouring into Boston until by midafternoon there were more than a thousand assembled. That afternoon the rebels prepared a declaration of intent that rehearsed all the wrongs that England had done them—heavy taxes, misappropriation of their property, institution of wars in which they had no interest and, above all, the "Popish Plot" that threatened the Protestant religion.

It was called "The Declaration of the Gentlemen, Merchants and Inhabitants of Boston and the Country Adjacent." If the title was hardly ringing, it was not quite yet the day of sloganeering, and the reading of this revolutionary paper sent thrills through the entire colony. For the intent was unmistakable; Boston and Massachusetts colony would no longer live under this tyranny.

Governor Andros was taken in chains to the fort, which had been captured by the rebels. Most of his high officials also were held prisoner there or confined to the common jail. In two days the revolution was completed and a Committee of Safety took over the rule of the colony. At the head of it was Simon Bradstreet, former royal governor. For the next few months the rule of Massachusetts was actually in the hands of the people.

Under James II, the old colonies had been disbanded, and Rhode Island and Connecticut had been joined with Massachusetts and Plymouth in "the Dominion." Now all were suddenly free in the confusion of the change of rulers in London.

Plymouth came under the rule of its old governor and councillors. Rhode Islanders seized Andros' man, Joseph Dudley, and sent him off to the Boston jail; but there was no figure to emerge here (or in Boston for that matter) who exercised real leadership, and so the colony struggled without much government until William began to pay attention to what was happening across the sea.

Connecticut was in the throes of real revolution, harboring a party led by James Fitch, which had the most alarming "democratick" tendencies. But the Tories managed to quiet affairs and soon quelled such rebellion.

In New York, also a part of the "Dominion," Suffolk County on Long Island was first to rebel. Then came Setauket. And on May 30 rebellion erupted in New York City in a violent argument between the governor's redcoats and the city's militia over the posting of a sentry. In the dispute Lieutenant Governor Nicholson threatened to pistol-whip a militiaman.

That threw the fat into the fire. Captain Jacob Leisler, a German from Frankfurt who had been a merchant in New York for twenty years, reverted to his old calling and emerged as commander of the rebel soldiers who flocked about him.

On June 8 the rebels elected a Committee of Safety, and a few days later Governor Nicholson fled to England to report on the treason endemic in America.

On July 16 John Goode and an army of Protestants marched on St. Mary's in the name of the rebellion and seized the State House and forthwith published a long declaration, which was more a justification than a rebellious charter.

By August the revolutionaries had called a representative assembly, which met in the last week of the month, and this local government managed colonial affairs in Maryland while waiting for William III to pay attention to his western colonies.

In New York, the revolutionary government lasted until 1691, when the new governor, Colonel Henry Sloughter, arrived to take charge in the name of William III. Sloughter's prime claim to fame was the fact that he had been one of the first to welcome Prince Henry back to English soil from his exile on the continent. Thus were governors made.

The new governor immediately demanded surrender of

the revolutionary power, and since he had the redcoats and the power of the king behind him, the end was inevitable. Leisler was arrested and clapped into jail, and New York was once again a royal colony under strict control of England.

Massachusetts, led by Increase Mather, tried to hold out for local autonomy, power for the legislature, and virtual independence of the governor. In the end the Bay Staters won some rights, and Massachusetts, almost alone among royal colonies, had the power in the lower house to elect its own governor's council, subject to the governor's approval. The new charter also granted to Massachusetts men all the liberties and immunities of free Englishmen.

Jacob Leisler and nine others were tried in New York and found guilty of treason, and he and seven others were sentenced to be hanged, disemboweled, decapitated, and quartered. Finally Leisler and one other were hanged and their heads struck off.

But in the months that had passed, the new governor had learned that Leisler was not forgotten, and so in the Spring of 1691 when the people demanded virtual reenactment of the Charter of Libertyes of 1683, they got it. The governor could read the temper of the people. The supreme legislative power was to reside in the governor, council, and "the people."

In Maryland, John Goode escaped as the representatives of the king arrived, and went to England where he poisoned the atmosphere against Lord Baltimore and cost him his colony. Maryland was made a royal colony, several of Goode's supporters were appointed to the council, and soon the legislature had passed a liberalized charter.

But in the end virtually all these changes were nullified by the king in London, who asserted the royal prerogative

56

to govern the colonies as king's colonies. But the principle that Americans were as good as Englishmen and should have all the same rights and privileges was firmly established in the minds of the leaders of the new world.

In the Spring of 1698 the Earl of Bellomont came to New York as the new governor, and from his studies of the Leisler case, he concluded that Leisler and his fellow convict had been "barbarously murdered" in the name of the crown. With the governor's blessing, the families of the men exhumed the bodies and gave them Christian burials in the Dutch church that autumn. Although a terrible storm blew for three days, twelve hundred New Yorkers showed up for the most impressive funeral held in that colony in all its years.

New York had not forgotten the Glorious Revolution.

11

The Politicking of
William Penn

If William Penn's father had not been one of the most
prominent defenders of the crown in the middle of the
seventeenth century, it is doubtful Penn would have survived or at least prospered enough to achieve his dream
of a colony on the American shore dedicated to religious
liberty.

But Vice Admiral William Penn commanded the Irish
fleet in the Dutch war and then went, for Cromwell, to
the West Indies. What happened there is rather muddy in
history, but when he came back he was clapped into the
Tower, and then, when Charles II was restored to his
throne, the admiral was honored with a knighthood and
appointed as commissioner of the navy.

Young William, born in 1644 in London, was a great
disappointment to his father, for he used his fine education to develop the oddest nonconformist ideas. Indeed,

although he went up to Oxford in 1660, he went down again in 1661, rejected for "nonconformity," which in his case meant objections to the compulsory chapel service and the ideas of the prayer book of the Church of England.

The admiral sent William off on the Grand Tour of Europe, hoping that travel would overcome the oddness. It persisted and grew worse. He was sent to Ireland to manage his father's estates and proved, in this, a skinflint type who did very well.

And then he capped it all by joining the Society of Friends, those nonconformists who objected to taxation for defense, oath taking, and other common practices of the realm. William not only joined, he became an ardent worker. Even as a boy he had strange tendencies (he had his first "mystical" experience when he was twelve) and at twenty-six found himself in the dock charged with "preaching to the people."

In a way he made political history even then. Educated and articulate, he argued well before the court and convinced the jury that he and his friends were innocent of wrongdoing. And in spite of mistreatment by the court (held overnight without food, drink, or beds) the jurors stubbornly held their verdict. Not guilty, they said.

So furious was Judge Sir Samuel Starling, also Mayor of London, that he arrested the whole jury!

This act created a furor, caused the crown to step in and protect juries from angry judges in the future, and made William Penn a famous man, although he was put into jail despite the jury's verdict and held in Newgate prison. He spent his time writing tracts and diatribes and being tried for the next few months.

He was deeply involved in the religious quarrels of the day (the Popish Plot of the 1670s) and his struggle for religious liberty was as unceasing as it was ubiquitous, for in this guise he concerned himself with such matters as government by Parliament, freedom of trade, personal industry, and the rights of property.

It was influence and his father's reputation that gained him Pennsylvania. He was granted these royal lands in America and secured a charter for their management and government under the crown. His payment to the king was to be two beaver skins a year. Considering that he got in return the right to appoint magistrates, govern, make laws with the assistance of an assembly, establish a judicial system, make war on enemies, levy taxes, dispose of lands—it was a very good bargain.

And so William Penn came to America.

The government he established was a liberal one for its time, notable among other matters for its enlightened judicial system in which the punishment fit the crime. Justice, said Penn, "shall neither be sold, denied or delayed."

In America he immediately quarreled with Lord Baltimore (which spoke loudly for Penn's liberality) and he was forever having the difficulties of dukedoms with the boundaries of his fief.

Back in England in the middle of the 1680s, he found he got on well with King James II, and he secured through the crown the release and relief of many Quakers who had been imprisoned in England.

His own government was not particularly notable for equanimity of action. He quarreled with his governors and his councils and experimented with authoritarianism. The abdication of James and the accession of King William put an end to Penn's prominence in England. Thereafter his main interest was in keeping Pennsylvania's name out of the newspapers, lest the new king take too great an interest in it and seize the land in the name of the crown.

But in 1696 Penn, who was always apt with ideas, produced one that was to have far-reaching consequences on the North American continent. It was, as he put it, "A Brief and Plain Scheme How the English Colonies in the North parts of America . . . may be made more useful to the Crown and one another's peace and safety with an universal concurrence."

It was, in other words, a simple plan for a simple sort of union.

"The colonies," said Penn, "should send two deputies for each colony to some central meeting place—say New York—to debate and resolve such measures as are most advisable for their better understanding and their perfect tranquility and safety." The chairman of these meetings would be some person commissioned by the king, perhaps the governor of New York. This assembly would adjust all matters in dispute between the several colonies. Majority vote would rule.

There were many matters that pressed harder each year. For example, the extradition of criminals. A counterfeiter might operate in Connecticut, and when pursued, flee to North Carolina. How were the Connecticut authorities to pursue him? Now, in 1696 it was virtually impossible. But by simple agreement of extradition, the accused could be hauled back to Connecticut to face his accusers.

Then there was the problem of intercolonial commerce. Who would manage such affairs? A merchant in Boston might have orders for pewter ware from Virginia, but dare he ship and bill? Who was to make certain that he was able to collect, and how would common carriers, or peddlers, for that matter, be regulated? There were many pressing problems regarding trade that demanded mutual attention by the colonies.

Penn, like many another in the American colonies, had realized that the people on this shore of the Atlantic were bound together by events and mutual problems far more than they were to England.

61

In the matter of supporting what Penn called "the union and safety" of the provinces against public enemies, there must be joint action. This, for the most part, meant the French and Indians. If there was to be defense, how much money should be put up by each colony and how many men must be supplied?

Only such an assembly could decide on such knotty points unless they wished to throw all these questions to London and let the crown decide, which was dangerous because the crown might not get around to deciding at all, and if such decisions were made, they could very well be capricious.

London did not care much for Penn's idea of unity in America. Divide and conquer was London's policy; when people in far-off places got together the results were not usually salutary to the crown.

But Penn persisted in this scheme, and in 1700 he had managed to hold meetings with Governor Bellomont of New York, Governor Nicholson of Virginia, and Governor Hamilton of New Jersey.

They were setting up plans for the establishment of a colonial mint to make coins for all the colonies. This would be a great boon to merchants; they now suffered too much from counterfeiters and clippers, the latter being dishonest fellows who clipped off bits of the silver and copper coins and then sold the clippings as precious metals, still passing the coins at their original value. They were also joined by borers who hollowed out silver coins and gold ones and filled the interiors with base metals. And so a merchant's patience and his teeth were often tried in commerce.

Penn had drawn several proposals, one for the apprehension and punishment of runaways and debtors. And then there was the problem of naturalization.

For example, a Spaniard from the Floridas might take

a liking to Virginia colony and settle there. He might want to buy property and become a free holder. The rules in Virginia for this had no bearing on what Maryland was doing next door, and in the settlement of estates and other matters there was much confusion. Penn realized as did few others how inseparably bound the colonies had become by the matter of geography and mutual ties.

Also, although this aspect was best not emphasized in contact with London, the governors, acting in concert, could have more influence on Parliament and the Privy Council in matters they wanted adjusted in London. They did want and asked for adjustment of the Navigation Acts, to give persons who helped in capture of pirates a part of the booty and thus discourage the rude practice of people helping the pirates who gave them a share of the plunder. They also wanted easement of restrictions in the Woolen Act, which prohibited colonial manufacture of woolen cloth (in behalf of London's woolen mills) and forced the colonists to import their clothing.

There was also the question of timber. America had vast quantities of timber. It was one of the continent's major resources. And yet, while London was eager to protect London merchants in such matters as wool, the central government gave no encouragement to the colonies in such matters as timber. By simply placing an import duty on foreign timber, the crown could assure the prosperity of the colonials.

Penn, of course, was not acting disinterestedly. He was at that moment having serious troubles in Pennsylvania. For one thing the Quakers were a stubborn lot, and they refused either to participate or contribute in general defense against the Indians who were marauding on the western end of the colony. A colonial assembly with general participation and adherence could force the unwilling Quakers to do their duty more easily than could Penn.

There was also the problem of too much paperwork. Everything had to be sent to London for approval. If London would grant a general assembly the right to decide the matters, how much easier it would be for the crown to manage the colonies, and how much easier for the individual colonies to manage relations with London.

But the king and his ministers were not interested in efficiency. They knew the sources of control, and they possessed the power to tax and the power to raise arms. They had no intention in 1700 of relinquishing those powers to local authority in New York or anywhere else in America.

And so Penn's scheme for what was no more nor less than a Continental Congress in 1696 came to nothing at all except to further his acquaintance among his fellow colonial officials.

12

The Charter of Privileges

In many ways Pennsylvania was a symbol of colonial enlightenment. But not entirely because of William Penn, who, in spite of his activities in his own behalf, was primarily the "proprietor" trying to make his colony a successful enterprise for himself.

By 1700, when the crown turned down his efforts to establish a union of the colonies, Penn was disgruntled and discouraged. He had been right that cooperative effort would have been the best method of securing mutual defense, but he learned now, as if he did not know before, that being right is no excuse. The crown would have its way.

The dangers that Penn predicted came to pass soon enough. In 1700 there were rumors, even reaching London, that the French were outfitting a fleet to send to the new world to help conquer the territories there. That was not comforting to London. Then came others that the Indians on Lord Bellomont's borders of New York were in an uprising, and that was equally disquieting. Of course they had been harrying Penn's folk for years.

So instead of mutual effort, Penn soon had a bill from William III for £350 to contribute to the general defense of America. Penn sent it posthaste to the Pennsylvania assembly, where it was greeted with groans and shouts of anger. The colony was still too young to pay such monstrous bills, said the assemblymen, and they could not afford it. Would Penn please tell that to the king?

And furthermore, let Penn tell the assembly that as Quakers they had religious scruples against such activity.

Although Penn agreed with them in principle, one of the responsibilities he had agreed also to undertake when he had the charter that gave him the colony was to defend it. And now if he would not defend it, or contribute to the defense, he could imagine what William III's reaction would be.

He was right. The stalling had angered William and his Privy Council, and in 1701 a bill was presented to Parliament to bring proprietary governments under control. That did not mean buying out the proprietors; it meant taking over their authority.

Obviously, such a monstrosity was not to be encouraged, and Penn fought. He was at some disadvantage because he was in America at the time, but he sent a petition to his son William, Jr., who stopped his dalliances and his wine-bibbing long enough to present it at court.

But the quarrel continued, and in 1703 Penn said he had had enough and tried to sell Pennsylvania to the king. But the king was short of money, and some counsellors suggested that it was foolish to buy something that might be seized at any moment. The crown offered a cut-rate price and Penn refused. So much for the going price of America!

As if these difficulties were not enough, the colonists were giving Penn troubles.

The basic problem was that the Pennsylvanians were a polyglot lot. The Quakers had come with Penn, but the freedom of the colony had attracted Swedes, Irish, and Germans, and the dissenters from every other colony. So by 1700 Pennsylvania very definitely represented a mixed bag in every department: religious, political, racial, cultural.

Such a group would have different ideas on just about every aspect of life and society, and they did. They shared one activity: pressing against William Penn to remove the authority over their lives and property and put it in their hands.

So Penn was beset from above and below. The crown insisted that he make his payments; the people refused. The crown threatened; the people threatened.

He had trouble with squatters who invaded his proprietary lands, refused to pay rent, and would not leave.

As if that were not enough to vex even the most liberal capitalist, Penn was also beset by his legislators. He had appointed a governor to manage the affairs of the colony earlier when he sailed for a long stay in England. The governor was told to select an advisory council and would have appointive and judicial powers. Also, the governor could summon the legislative body for the making of laws.

And so in Penn's long absence, little by little, the assembly had taken power away from the governor and the proprietor of the colony.

Thus, in the last half of the 1690s, when Penn was back in America, the assembly held that it now had the power to make the laws. Penn's new governor, William Markham, dissolved both the assembly and the council and then had the temerity to appoint a new council, although the charter called for election.

The people were furious, and in the fall of 1696, when Penn saw that something had to be done to strengthen defense of the frontiers, Markham called a special assembly for the purpose. The assembly refused to pass a money bill to raise funds for defense unless Penn and his governor did something about the laws.

Governor Markham then allowed the assembly to frame a constitution giving that body the right to initiate legislation. It was never accepted by Penn and therefore did not become law. The importance of it is in its reflection of the strong ideas of the colonists even before 1700.

In 1701, when Penn wanted to go back to England to pursue his own aims, fight the antiproprietary movement in England, and argue for his all-colony union, he relented in his relations with the people.

"Since all men are mortal," he declared, he would be willing to adjust the charter under which they were governed in any reasonable method. Obviously he felt it doubtful that he would ever return to Pennsylvania.

And so the colonists of Pennsylvania had their Charter of Privileges. A unicameral legislature was established (a unique idea in the colonies) and it had the right to choose its own officers, including the speaker. It could judge its own qualifications and those of members. And it provided for "all other powers and privileges of an assembly according to the rights of the free born subjects of England and as is usual in any of the King's plantations in America."

Penn then left, never to return to Pennsylvania.

13

Pattern for a Kingdom

In later years Thomas Jefferson would call him the finest stylist of the English language and would revere his political ideas as much as he did those of any man. At the age of thirty-three, he was secretary of state in the English government, and he would go down in history as the epitome of the humanism of the eighteenth century.

He was born Henry St. John in 1678 at Battersea, but he was to be known to the world later as Lord Bolingbroke.

St. John's father, known in society as Old Frumps, was a man dedicated to the pleasures of the world. But the boy did not take after his father and indeed had little to do with him in his life. He was educated at Eton College, which automatically set him apart from average men. But that did not account for the influence he was to hold in the English social changes of his day.

St. John's education was completed by a tour of the continent, where in 1698 he was to be found in Paris and later studying civil law at Geneva. Here were sowed the seeds of his political ideals.

In the study of Roman law, young St. John saw clearly a commitment to public order. This was to develop into a thorough commitment to the responsibility and authority of Parliament and a distaste for what he called "the moneyed interest" that had so large an influence in the government of England.

He went to Parliament shortly after the turn of the century and almost immediately became a leader in the House. He was deeply involved in machinations to press the succession of James Francis Edward, son of James II, to succeed the aging Queen Anne, but he lost out and George I, from the other side of the House of Windsor, became the king in 1714, whereupon St. John fled to the continent. His politicking had been too brazen for him to continue to live in England.

By this time St. John had become Viscount Bolingbroke, as he would be known after 1712. He spent the next nine years on the continent, largely in France, where he mingled with such important political figures as Voltaire. And on his return to England, pardoned for his political crimes, he began his most important period in politics as far as the molding of American thought was concerned.

He was to organize the opposition to the Walpole government into an effective force and to develop a theory of Parliamentary opposition that was to have a lasting effect on the rights of Englishmen, and thus the claimed rights of Americans.

Bolingbroke's view was that the king's function in legislative matters was purely negative. He advanced the theory of the separation of powers of the monarch, or "supreme magistrate" as he called him, and those of the Houses of Parliament.

These ideas were sharpened by his time in Parliament; then in 1735, Bolingbroke again retired to France to reflect on the theories derived from his practical experience in politics.

He then began his major political work, *The Idea of a Patriot King*, which, when finally published in 1749, was to make a deep impression in England and across the Atlantic.

This book was a rejection of the theory of the divine right of monarchy. Society, he held, must be a partnership between governor and governed. There must be limitations on the power of the crown so as to secure the liberties of the people. Otherwise, the monarchy became a tyranny.

And this, suggested Bolingbroke, was what was happening in England under the first two Georges, the Hanoverians who had cast their lot with the moneyed and landed element of English society.

Thus, as the colonists of North America considered what they believed to be the mistreatment they were receiving from their mother country, they had in Bolingbroke's writings a rationale for the criticism of the king.

That idea would be very important in shaping political thought on the western shore of the Atlantic, for the farther from the seat of power that the ideas were discussed, the more they gained in prominence.

It was no accident that Jefferson's thinking was influenced by Bolingbroke's writings.

14

The Spirit of Laws

Not all the political ideas that affected the American colonists originated in England or from the English tradition. During this same period of the eighteenth century, French political thought was also in ferment, and out of it would come a number of important ideas for consideration in the Americas.

Charles de Montesquieu was one of the restless intellectuals of the European continent. He was well-to-do, almost a requisite for one who would find the leisure to study and develop thoughtful ideas. He was born in 1689, and in 1728 he gave up the world of affairs, set out on a long trip around Europe, which included a stay in England, and then settled down to write his major work, *The Spirit of Laws*.

Montesquieu's study was governments and their behavior, and he ranged from Ancient Rome to contemporary China and back again to Europe.

In a sense Montesquieu's work is important because of the whole, the sum of the parts, rather than for the individual parts themselves. He considered the relations of men under government in all its aspects in all the world, modern and ancient.

In relation to monarchy, he advanced the theory that monarchy became corrupt when the prince insensibly deprived the society of its privileges. Montesquieu had no great love for "democracy." He noted with a cynical satisfaction its failure in the Cromwellian period in England and how that nation had to return to the monarchy it had abandoned.

But he did have a basic understanding of all the important factors of government, the interrelationship between liberty, equality of punishment, reasonableness of taxation, and the importance of commerce.

And in Book XI he warned of the need to guard freedom. "Political liberty is to be found only in moderate governments, and even in these it is not always. It is there only when there is no abuse of power. But constant experience shows us that every man invested with power is apt to abuse it and to carry his authority as far as it will go. . . .

"To prevent this abuse, it is necessary from the very nature of things that power should be a check to power. A government may be so constituted as no man shall be compelled to do things to which the law does not oblige him nor forced to abstain from things which the law permits."

And Montesquieu offered food for thought with this idea:

"Again there is no liberty if the judiciary power be not

73

separated from the legislative and executive. Were it joined with the legislative, the life and liberty of the subject would be exposed to arbitrary control, for the judge would be then the legislator. Were it joined to the executive power, the judge might behave with violence and repression."

There is a tendency of many Americans in the twentieth century to believe that the political processes and the concepts of liberty and good government somehow sprang fullblown from the seeds of the American Revolution. But as Montesquieu's calm, encylopedic study of political institutions indicates, intelligent Europeans were well aware of differing philosophies of government.

In fact, Montesquieu was, one might say, bitten by the "English bug." He returned from England disliking many English traits, but entirely wedded to the basic institutions of England. He recognized that with all its faults England had the most free and representative government in Europe and, in its way, the most stable.

Montesquieu's book could, in the final analysis, be read as a virtual endorsement of the English system. When it was completed in the 1740s, he showed it to a number of friends on the continent, and they were unanimous in their advice that he forget it and abandon the idea of publication.

But Montesquieu stubbornly insisted that it would be published, and in 1748 it was brought out in Geneva.

On the continent, and particularly in France, the book was greeted by the critics with the most unfriendly remarks possible. They did not like Montesquieu's point of view nor his reiteration of a theme: the interdependence of all persons who live in a land and must suffer government of some sort.

In London, however, the work was greeted with high

enthusiasm and respect that grew into something akin to awe. When Montesquieu died a few years later, the London *Evening Post* lamented his death, calling him "a friend to mankind."

15

The Revolutionism of
Jean Jacques Rousseau

The eighteenth century was alive with political ideas, and
one of the most revolutionary thinkers of the time was
Jean Jacques Rousseau, born in Geneva in 1712, but
more properly a citizen of France, where he chose to
spend his most productive years.

He wandered about Europe, observing and working at
various tasks, and in 1743 decided to write a book on
"political institutions." This was the year in which
Thomas Jefferson was born.

Nineteen years later, when Rousseau had been writing
for twenty years and establishing his reputation, he published *The Social Contract,* perhaps his most famous
work, and one which so affected European political thinking that it worried the French royal authorities. Rousseau
fled into exile just ahead of arrest and then continued

from one place to another to write his controversial essays.

In 1766 Rousseau went to England with David Hume, which gave him a certain cachet in addition to his own reputation.

He had studied inequality among men and wrote a treatise on the origin of inequality, pointing out that no man has a natural authority over any other. In other words, while men are different and unequal physically or naturally, there is an equality that is moral and legitimate. Men who are unequal in strength or intelligence all become equal by convention and legal right.

This work paved the way for his most famous writing, *The Social Contract*, which studies the relationship between men and government.

To Rousseau government was: "An intermediate body set up between the subjects and the Sovereign to secure their mutual correspondence, charged with the execution of the laws and the maintenance of liberty, both civil and political."

Among the ideas that Rousseau developed was the dissolution of the State.

"When the Prince ceases to administer the State in accordance with the laws, and usurps the Sovereign power, a remarkable change then occurs. Not the government, but the State undergoes contraction: I mean that the great State is dissolved and another is formed within it, composed solely of the members of the government, which becomes for the rest of the people merely master and tyrant. So that the moment the government usurps the Sovereignty, the social compact is broken and all private citizens recover by right their natural liberty and are forced, but not bound, to obey.

". . . royalty degenerates into tyranny . . ."

This work, like *Discours sur l'inégalité*, created a literary sensation throughout Europe. The former book had made Rousseau's name famous in England. It also identified him with the cult of the "noble savage," the concept of idealization of "natural man." (Jefferson and many others on the American continent were deeply impressed by the concept of the natural nobility of mankind, as can be seen in the Declaration of Independence.)

But the second work, greater in its scope, aroused a storm of protest and anger in England. Edmund Burke, for example, found it extremely dangerous, for it revealed to the people the full extent of their power. If the concept took hold, and they acted on it, they could force upon the government whatever drastic change in theory they wished.

Burke was upset from the beginning from those opening words of Rousseau's:

"Man is born free; and everywhere he is in chains. . . ."

Those words, those ideas, were anathema to a politician who wished to be successful in the England of George II (and the same would hold true of the England of George III).

16

The Egalitarianism of
Cesare Beccaria

Cesare Beccaria, Marchese di Bonesana, was a man born
with a silver spoon in his mouth if there ever was one. He
came from a wealthy noble family of Milan, and he grew
up hawking and riding, and chasing peasant girls, between
drinking and feasting bouts.

For years his family lamented his ways, but he soon
steadied down and acquired a doctorate in law at the University of Padua and became immersed in the intellectual
life of the period.

These were the days of the Enlightenment, the years of
the eighteenth century when men of all nations were ex-
ploring the universes about them in terms of natural law
and new philosophies of the nature of things. They had
cast off the narrow strictures imposed on intellectual life
by the church.

And in this, Beccaria undertook a most unusual sort of

study. When he was twenty-six he published his book on crimes and punishments, a field in which no real scholar had hitherto ventured. His study was a symbol of the growing interest of Europeans in the way in which society worked.

Beccaria's work was soon translated into English, and was widely acclaimed in Europe, where it created an enormous amount of interest. It made its way across the Atlantic to the new world, and indeed, was well read in Pennsylvania and served as a model in the modification of that colony's judicial codes.

If it seems odd that one of the major works of political thought that affected men on the American continent was devoted to crime and punishment, the fact is that in the still arbitrary nature of European society few men dared write openly on the rights of the people as opposed to the rights of authority.

Cesare Beccaria's book is notable for the breadth of its subject. It deals with the origin of punishments and the right to punish, with the whole idea of imprisonment, with secret accusations, oaths, banishment, confiscations, the death penalty, mercy, and virtually every other concept that comes into play in crime and the punishment of crime.

But more than that, Beccaria's work espoused the principle that legislation ought to be directed to the end of procuring the greatest happiness to be shared by the greatest number of people.

And while this was not the case in governments, it was the ideal to which governments ought to strive.

The political community needed readjustment: it ought to be the result of an accord entered into by men in order to guarantee for themselves the maximum enjoyment of personal liberty.

Each individual willingly sacrifices to the community

only so much liberty as "suffices others to defend it," Beccaria wrote.

Again, from another angle, Beccaria then approached the theory of the social contract. Laws should be conditions established under the social contract, and punishments ought to be given only to defend the sum of the sacrificed shares of liberty against private usurpation by individuals. Any other reason for punishment was unjust.

In its way, Beccaria's work was an indictment of the whole European governmental scene. Specifically, it was a plea against abuse of authority and aristocratic privilege, which caused so much irritation in America.

If government wants to prevent crimes, Beccaria said, the way is to be sure that the laws are clear and simple and the entire force of the nation united in their defense, and that no part of it is employed to destroy them.

Laws must not favor classes of men as men themselves. Men should fear laws and nothing else.

And this:

"Another way of preventing crimes is to direct the interest of the magistracy as a whole to observance rather than corruption of the laws. The greater the number of magistrates, the less dangerous is the abuse of legal power. Venality is more difficult among men who observe one another, and their interest in increasing their personal authority diminishes as the portion that would fall to each is less, especially in comparison with the danger involved in the undertaking. If the Sovereign, with his apparatus and pomp, with the severity of his edicts, with the permission he grants for unjust as well as just claims to be advanced by anyone who thinks himself oppressed, accustoms his subjects to fear magistrates more than laws (the magistrates) will profit more from this fear than personal and public security will gain from it."

The indictment, then, was of the sovereigns or the aristocracy, the men of wealth and circumstance whose selfish interests seemed to rule in this period of history in Europe and America.

Beccaria was, in other words, censuring governments for their refusal to behave in the interests of most of the people. He vented his anger against all the rulers, legislators, jurists, magistrates, policemen, and jailers of the time.

And in 1770 came a point of application for Beccaria's words and reasoning.

On March 1 of that year, two British regiments were quartered in Boston, a part of King George's effort to intimidate the colonists against protests of his manner of governing. The 29th Regiment was quartered in barracks just south of King Street, and its presence was not welcomed by Boston citizens. That day there were fights on Grey's ropewalk not far from the barracks. For the next four days there were other fights and many threats uttered between townspeople and soldiers. On the fifth day, a crowd of citizens were standing in Dock Square listening to a harangue from a "mysterious stranger" when "a company of lawless boys" began harrying the sentry, who was pacing his beat before the customhouse.

Earlier in the evening the sentry had pushed a barber's apprentice who was speaking insolently to a captain of the 14th Regiment, and this boy was in the crowd claiming injury and inciting his fellows to mob the sentry.

They began throwing ice balls at him, and when other soldiers came up they assaulted them, too. Henry Knox, the bookseller, came up, as did Captain Preston of the regiment, and Knox persuaded Preston to refrain from firing on the mob. The noise grew louder, the crowd more menacing, and somehow one soldier discharged his musket, whereupon so did others. Three people were killed and eight wounded.

In the weeks that followed, Samuel Adams raised to new heights of fury the temper of the people of Boston. The "Boston Massacre" trial was delayed for months as Boston clamored for English blood.

And when it came, Sam Adams' cousin John was one of the lawyers for the defense.

He opened with a quotation from Beccaria:

"If, by defending the rights of man and of unconquerable truth, I should help to save from the spasm and agonies of death some wretched victim of tyranny or of no less fatal ignorance, the thanks and tears of one innocent mortal in his transports of joy would console me for the contempt of all mankind."

It was England, the crown, injustice that were on trial here, and not the soldiers who were no more than the dupes of tyranny. That thought had been planted in Milan by Beccaria, and it grew in the fertile soil of Boston.

17

Benjamin Franklin's Dream

Benjamin Franklin was forty-five years old before he ever gave much consideration to politics. That in itself is remarkable; consider that Bolingbroke was in Parliament in his twenties and a senior minister of the crown in his thirties, and that most of the other political figures of the time had come to that sphere of interest early.

In a way, then, Franklin's late appearance was a phenomenon. In another way it was a natural outgrowth of all the experiences he had enjoyed, for as writer and printer, editor, reporter, what-have-you in the field of the public word, Franklin had always been on the fringes of politics.

Since 1736 he had served as clerk of the assembly, but from his viewpoint that was largely for business purposes. Yet it exposed him at close hand to the vagaries of politics and to the ideas of his fellows in Philadelphia.

Franklin brought one shining aspect to public affairs: he was one of the few colonists in the political sphere who was not a man of rank and wealth. He was strictly middle class; his mother had been born on Nantucket Island in an egalitarian society. He grew up in Boston and learned to work with his hands as a printer in his brother's shop. Only later did he write some of those articles he printed, and through his political essays (which got his brother jailed) he learned the power of the printed word.

In comparison, remember that Thomas Jefferson, that wellborn son of Virginia, was a burgess at the age of twenty-five, and George Washington at the age of twenty-six. Nothing could be more in contrast than the careers of these aristocrats and that of Benjamin Franklin, the self-made man.

As such, he espoused the cause of the middle class. In 1747 he had published *Plain Truth,* a pamphlet addressed to shopkeepers and farmers. He pointed out to them that unlike the rich they could not pick up and leave the land if they were threatened from abroad. And thus (with the French and Indian troubles as background), when he proposed the formation of a citizen's army or militia, ten thousand Pennsylvanians subscribed. Franklin, tubby, near-sighted, middle-aged burgher, narrowly escaped being made colonel of the regiment.

For years Franklin had opposed the more oppressive of the crown's limitations of the economic freedom of the colonists. He was, indeed, an entirely practical man. For example, the sort of thing that truly aroused his ire was the Parliament's Iron Act of 1750, which forbade the building of new forges and slitting mills in the colonies but encouraged the export of unprocessed iron. The point of that law, of course, was to bleed the colonies, push them into sending their iron to England for working, and then buy back the tools from the mother country. It was of a piece with the Woolen Act, which had the same effect on clothing.

Franklin could understand the English reasoning that held the colonies, in exchange for support and protection by England; and therefore should accept certain regulations. When England ruled that French manufactured goods should proceed to the colonies by way of London, that was understandable. Where Franklin then drew the line was in arbitrary and punitive regulations that made little difference to London but were matters of great moment in America.

In other words, Franklin was never against the idea of "Empire." He simply insisted that the Empire should be mutually supporting and that the Englishman living on American shores was every bit as much an Englishman and entitled to the same rights as the Englishman who lived in London or Somerset.

So fundamental was that belief that it was often forgotten in the arguments that developed in America after the 1760s.

But we are considering now the Franklin of the 1750s and the problems that had arisen on the North American continent. Primary of these was the threat from the French and the Indians whose cherished mutual desire it was to drive the English out altogether.

The difficulty in Pennsylvania was that the Quakers would not rouse to the danger that threatened. Secure in their faith, certain that pacifism would set all right in the future, they believed confidently that they had the friendship of the Indians. That is why Ben Franklin's idea for defense of the colony was the only possible manner in which it could be accomplished.

As did few other men in the colonies, Franklin saw the future of America. After projecting the rate of population

Hamilton delin.   Noble sculp.

The Manner *in which the* American Colonies *Declared themselves*
INDEPENDANT *of the* King *of* ENGLAND,
throughout the different Provinces, on July 4.1776.

Richard Hooker (1553–1600)
English philosopher, author of *The Laws of Ecclesiastical Polity*, and among the first to bring new ideas to the discus-

John Locke (1632–1704)
English political philosopher; his *Treatises on Government* and other writings were very influential in early American

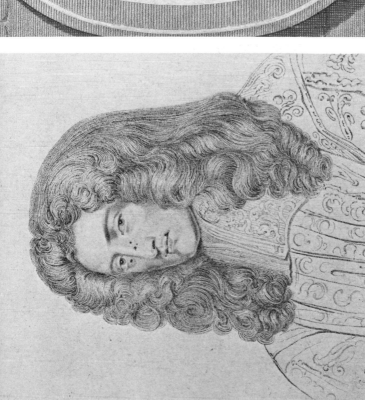

Anthony Ashley Cooper, Earl of Shaftesbury (1621–1683) An English statesman, he was deeply interested in the colonies and their growth. A close friend of Locke, he was responsible for the passage of England's famous Habeas Corpus Act in 1679.

Charles de Montesquieu (1689–1755) French lawyer, political thinker, and restless intellectual, his *Spirit of Laws* was a major work of the century and highly regarded in the colonies.

Jean Jacques Rousseau (1712–1778)
One of Europe's most revolutionary thinkers and author of the famed work, *The Social Contract*, which studied the

Edmund Burke (1729–1797)
Outspoken English statesman and orator, he repeatedly urged the Crown to give the colonists the same rights as all

Henry St. John, Lord Bolingbroke (1678–1733)
English political theorist and author of *The Idea of a Patriot King*. He was admired by Thomas Jefferson and his ideas adapted in the drafting of the Declaration.

William Penn (1644–1718)
Quaker founder of Pennsylvania and a champion of religious and political freedom in the colonies. He led the first attempt at a union of the colonies.

George Washington (1732–1799)
Commander-in-Chief of the Continental Army and first President of the
United States. For twenty tumultuous years he guided the fledgling nation

Thomas Jefferson (1743–1826)
Architect, lawyer, and literary man, he was chosen to draft the Declaration.
He later became Vice President (1796) and President (1801).

Thomas Paine (1737–1809)
Journalist and pamphleteer, his *Common Sense* was a spirited contribution to revolutionary thought in the colonies in early 1776.

Benjamin Franklin (1706–1790)
America's renaissance man, he was a late starter in politics but became an internationally renowned statesman and a major contributor to the Declaration.

Samuel Adams (1722–1803)
The most revolutionary of the colonists, he was called "a professional patriot and propagandist," though his fight for liberty was often at his personal expense.

John Adams (1735–1825)
"The Atlas of American Independence," he was a brilliant orator and a fiery figure in the days of the revolution. A vital contributor to the Declaration, he later became our second President.

One of Virginia's favorite sons, Patrick Henry, in an early event leading

olution . . . as he berates the Crown in his "Parson's Cause" speech in 1763.

Patrick Henry (1736–1799)
One of the most outspoken critics of the King and royal policies and a fiery speaker whose "Give me liberty or give me death" roused the colonists in 1775.

Richard Henry Lee (1730–1794)
Another great orator from Virginia, he was an aggressive patriot and his resolutions eventually led to the drafting of the Declaration.

John Hancock
(1737—1793)
The wealthy and flamboyant young President of Congress and the first to sign the Declaration in the most visible of autographs.

Benjamin Harrison
(1726—1791)
He was chairman of the Committee of the Whole and presided over the debates on the drafting and acceptance of the Declaration.

There were fifty-eight signers of the Declaration of Independence, which began on July 4, 1776. Little-known is the fact that it took years before all the signatures were affixed to the final engrossed parchment document. The following pages contain likenesses of some of the signers.

William Whipple, New Hampshire

Robert Treat Paine, Massachusetts

Stephen Hopkins, Rhode Island

Roger Sherman, Connecticut

Philip Livingston, New York

John Witherspoon, New Jersey

Robert Morris, Pennsylvania

George Read, Delaware

Samuel Chase, Maryland

Francis Lightfoot Lee, Virginia

William Hooper, North Carolina

Edward Rutledge, South Carolina   **Lyman Hall,** Georgia

John Trumbull, artist famed for his painting of the signing of the Declaration of Independence and other historic events of the period

John Dunlap, the Philadelphia printer who worked through the night of July 4, 1776, printing the first official text of the Declaration

The Declaration of Independence. John Trumbull's famed painting, a fictional re-creation of the events of July 4, 1776.

Congress Voting Independence. Edward Savage's engraving of the July 2, 1776, decision.

An early print depicting Jefferson, Franklin, and Hancock leaving Independence Hall after having signed the Declaration.

Resolved That these united colonies are and of right ought to be free and independant states; that they are absolved from all allegiance to the british crown and that all political connection between them and the state of great Britain is and ought to be totally dissolved

Report &c July 2. 1776.
No 5 The resolution for independency agreed to July 2. 1776

Richard Henry Lee's resolution, which became the
Continental Congress's Declaration.

The Graff house in Philadelphia, where Jefferson labored in June, 1776, drafting the Declaration.

An early engraving illustrating the signers of the Declaration.

An old souvenir poster containing a collection of the signers' signatures from the Declaration.

A Declaration by the Representatives of the UNITED STATES OF AMERICA, in General Congress assembled.

When in the course of human events it becomes necessary for one people to dissolve the political bands which have connected them with another, and to assume among the powers of the earth the separate and equal station to which the laws of nature & of nature's god entitle them, a decent respect to the opinions of mankind requires that they should declare the causes which impel them to the separation.

We hold these truths to be self-evident; that all men are created equal, that they are endowed by their creator with equal rights, that among these are life, liberty, & the pursuit of happiness; that to secure these rights, governments are instituted among men, deriving their just powers from the consent of the governed; that whenever any form of government becomes destructive of these ends, it is the right of the people to alter or to abolish it, & to institute new government, laying it's foundation on such principles & organising it's powers in such form, as to them shall seem most likely to effect their safety & happiness. prudence indeed will dictate that governments long established should not be changed for light & transient causes: and accordingly all experience hath shewn that mankind are more disposed to suffer while evils are sufferable, than to right themselves by abolishing the forms to which they are accustomed. but when a long train of abuses & usurpations [begun at a distinguished period & pursuing invariably the same object, evinces a design to reduce them under absolute Despotism, it is their right, it is their duty, to throw off such government & to provide new guards for their future security. such has been the patient sufferance of these colonies; & such is now the necessity which constrains them to expunge their former systems of government. the history of the present king of Great Britain is a history of unremitting injuries and usurpations, among which appears no solitary fact to contradict the uniform tenor of the rest but all have in direct object the establishment of an absolute tyranny over these states. to prove this, let facts be submitted to a candid world, for the truth of which we pledge a faith yet unsullied by falsehood.]

The first page from Jefferson's handwritten draft of the Declaration.

The copy of Dunlap's first printing of the Declaration as it appears attached to the Rough Journal of Congress.

A fanciful version of the Declaration printed in Boston in 1841, one of the many artistic renditions created and sold as patriotic mementos.

IN CONGRESS, JULY 4, 1776.

A DECLARATION

BY THE REPRESENTATIVES OF THE

UNITED STATES OF AMERICA,

IN GENERAL CONGRESS ASSEMBLED.

WHEN in the Course of human Events, it becomes neceſſary for one People to diſſolve the Political Bands which have connected them with another, and to aſſume among the Powers of the Earth, the ſeparate and equal Station to which the Laws of Nature and of Nature's God entitle them, a decent Reſpect to the Opinions of Mankind requires that they ſhould declare the cauſes which impel them to the Separation.

We hold theſe Truths to be ſelf-evident, that all Men are created equal, that they are endowed by their Creator with certain unalienable Rights, that among theſe are Life, Liberty, and the Purſuit of Happineſs——That to ſecure theſe Rights, Governments are inſtituted among Men, deriving their juſt Powers from the Conſent of the Governed, that whenever any Form of Government becomes deſtructive of theſe Ends, it is the Right of the People to alter or to aboliſh it, and to inſtitute new Government, laying its Foundation on ſuch Principles, and organizing its Powers in ſuch Form, as to them ſhall ſeem moſt likely to effect their Safety and Happineſs. Prudence, indeed, will dictate that Governments long eſtabliſhed ſhould not be changed for light and tranſient Cauſes; and accordingly all Experience hath ſhewn, that Mankind are more diſpoſed to ſuffer, while Evils are ſufferable, than to right themſelves by aboliſhing the Forms to which they are accuſtomed. But when a long Train of Abuſes and Uſurpations, purſuing invariably the ſame Object, evinces a Deſign to reduce them under abſolute Deſpotiſm, it is their Right, it is their Duty, to throw off ſuch Government, and to provide new Guards for their future Security. Such has been the patient Sufferance of theſe Colonies; and ſuch is now the Neceſſity which conſtrains them to alter their former Syſtems of Government. The Hiſtory of the preſent King of Great-Britain is a Hiſtory of repeated Injuries and Uſurpations, all having in direct Object the Eſtabliſhment of an abſolute Tyranny over theſe States. To prove this, let Facts be ſubmitted to a candid World.

He has refuſed his Aſſent to Laws, the moſt wholeſome and neceſſary for the public Good.

He has forbidden his Governors to paſs Laws of immediate and preſſing Importance, unleſs ſuſpended in their Operation till his Aſſent ſhould be obtained; and when ſo ſuſpended, he has utterly neglected to attend to them.

He has refuſed to paſs other Laws for the Accommodation of large Diſtricts of People, unleſs thoſe People would relinquiſh the Right of Repreſentation in the Legiſlature, a Right ineſtimable to them, and formidable to Tyrants only.

He has called together Legiſlative Bodies at Places unuſual, uncomfortable, and diſtant from the Depoſitory of their public Records, for the ſole Purpoſe of fatiguing them into Compliance with his Meaſures.

He has diſſolved Repreſentative Houſes repeatedly, for oppoſing with manly Firmneſs his Invaſions on the Rights of the People.

He has refuſed for a long Time, after ſuch Diſſolutions, to cauſe others to be elected; whereby the Legiſlative Powers, incapable of Annihilation, have returned to the People at large for their exerciſe; the State remaining in the mean time expoſed to all the Dangers of Invaſion from without, and Convulſions within.

He has endeavoured to prevent the Population of theſe States; for that Purpoſe obſtructing the Laws for Naturalization of Foreigners; refuſing to paſs others to encourage their Migrations hither, and raiſing the Conditions of new Appropriations of Lands.

He has obſtructed the Adminiſtration of Juſtice, by refuſing his Aſſent to Laws for eſtabliſhing Judiciary Powers.

He has made Judges dependent on his Will alone, for the Tenure of their Offices, and the Amount and Payment of their Salaries.

He has erected a Multitude of new Offices, and ſent hither Swarms of Officers to harraſs our People, and eat out their Subſtance.

He has kept among us, in Times of Peace, Standing Armies, without the conſent of our Legiſlatures.

He has affected to render the Military independent of and ſuperior to the Civil Power.

He has combined with others to ſubject us to a Juriſdiction foreign to our Conſtitution, and unacknowledged by our Laws; giving his Aſſent to their Acts of pretended Legiſlation:

For quartering large Bodies of Armed Troops among us:

For protecting them, by a mock Trial, from Puniſhment for any Murders which they ſhould commit on the Inhabitants of theſe States:

For cutting off our Trade with all Parts of the World:

For impoſing Taxes on us without our Conſent:

For depriving us, in many Caſes, of the Benefits of Trial by Jury:

For tranſporting us beyond Seas to be tried for pretended Offences:

For aboliſhing the free Syſtem of Engliſh Laws in a neighbouring Province, eſtabliſhing therein an arbitrary Government, and enlarging its Boundaries, ſo as to render it at once an Example and fit Inſtrument for introducing the ſame abſolute Rule into theſe Colonies:

For taking away our Charters, aboliſhing our moſt valuable Laws, and altering fundamentally the Forms of our Governments:

For ſuſpending our own Legiſlatures, and declaring themſelves inveſted with Power to legiſlate for us in all Caſes whatſoever.

He has abdicated Government here, by declaring us out of his Protection and waging War againſt us.

He has plundered our Seas, ravaged our Coaſts, burnt our Towns, and deſtroyed the Lives of our People.

He is, at this Time, tranſporting large Armies of foreign Mercenaries to compleat the Works of Death, Deſolation, and Tyranny, already begun with circumſtances of Cruelty and Perfidy, ſcarcely paralleled in the moſt barbarous Ages, and totally unworthy the Head of a civilized Nation.

He has conſtrained our fellow Citizens taken Captive on the high Seas to bear Arms againſt their Country, to become the Executioners of their Friends and Brethren, or to fall themſelves by their Hands.

He has excited domeſtic Inſurrections amongſt us, and has endeavoured to bring on the Inhabitants of our Frontiers, the mercileſs Indian Savages, whoſe known Rule of Warfare, is an undiſtinguiſhed Deſtruction, of all Ages, Sexes and Conditions.

In every ſtage of theſe Oppreſſions we have Petitioned for Redreſs in the moſt humble Terms: Our repeated Petitions have been anſwered only by repeated Injury. A Prince, whoſe Character is thus marked by every act which may define a Tyrant, is unfit to be the Ruler of a free People.

Nor have we been wanting in Attentions to our Britiſh Brethren. We have warned them from Time to Time of Attempts by their Legiſlature to extend an unwarrantable Juriſdiction over us. We have reminded them of the Circumſtances of our Emigration and Settlement here. We have appealed to their native Juſtice and Magnanimity, and we have conjured them by the Ties of our common Kindred to diſavow theſe Uſurpations, which, would inevitably interrupt our Connections and Correſpondence. They too have been deaf to the Voice of Juſtice and of Conſanguinity. We muſt, therefore, acquieſce in the Neceſſity, which denounces our Separation, and hold them, as we hold the reſt of Mankind, Enemies in War, in Peace, Friends.

We, therefore, the Repreſentatives of the UNITED STATES OF AMERICA, in GENERAL CONGRESS, Aſſembled, appealing to the Supreme Judge of the World for the Rectitude of our Intentions, do, in the Name, and by Authority of the good People of theſe Colonies, ſolemnly Publiſh and Declare, That theſe United Colonies are, and of Right ought to be, FREE AND INDEPENDENT STATES; that they are abſolved from all Allegiance to the Britiſh Crown, and that all political Connection between them and the State of Great-Britain, is and ought to be totally diſſolved; and that as FREE AND INDEPENDENT STATES, they have full Power to levy War, conclude Peace, contract Alliances, eſtabliſh Commerce, and to do all other Acts and Things which INDEPENDENT STATES may of right do. And for the ſupport of this Declaration, with a firm Reliance on the Protection of divine Providence, we mutually pledge to each other our Lives, our Fortunes, and our ſacred Honor.

Signed by ORDER and in BEHALF of the CONGRESS,

JOHN HANCOCK, PRESIDENT.

ATTEST.
CHARLES THOMSON, SECRETARY.

PHILADELPHIA: PRINTED BY JOHN DUNLAP.

The famous "lost" copy of the original Declaration that John Dunlap printed on July 4, 1776. It is now owned by Ira G. Corn, Jr., and Joseph P. Driscoll.

The familiar engrossed Declaration of Independence, as copied in pen on parchment by Timothy Matlack. It was readied for signing on August 2, 1776. It wasn't until five years later that the last signature was obtained!

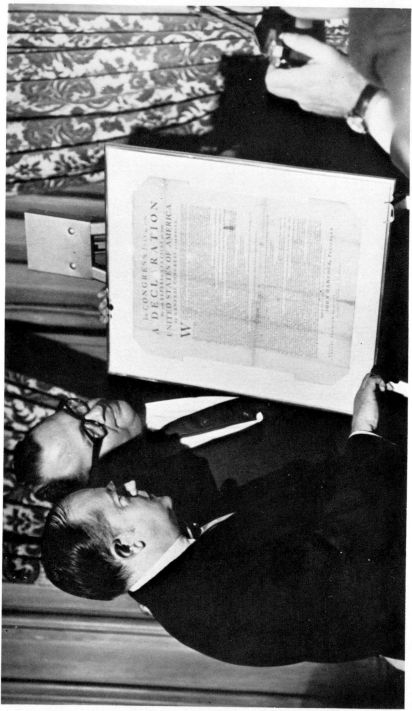

Driscoll and Corn with their copy of the Declaration shortly after their purchase of it for $404,000 in 1969. The Corn-Driscoll copy is now considered one of the most traveled of the Declarations extant, and was a major part of America's Bicentennial Celebration in 1976.

growth so much higher than that of Europe because of the availability of lands and the need for early marriages to provide "family power" to work them, he began speaking and writing of the time when America would be larger than England. Had those words been heeded, King George and his counselors might have trod a little softer in their policy toward America. But the trouble was that in this, as in so much else, Britain failed to understand the realities of life on the western shore of the great ocean.

The key to Franklin's dream of an expanded America was the constant push westward across the continent. That push was threatened in the 1750s by French and Indian pressure, and Franklin saw only one way to resist it. The English colonies must unite.

In the Spring of 1754, Virginia colony attempted to expand westward. Lieutenant Governor Robert Dinwiddie sent twenty-one-year-old George Washington to protest French moves into the Ohio country, and he returned to report that the French would not get out by persuasion. It would take force to drive them away.

Dinwiddie then sent Washington back to build a fort and hold the country. Washington fought the French but was defeated, and English expansion on the continent was threatened.

Up in Philadelphia, Franklin saw clearly the threat to the English colonies. On May 9 his Pennsylvania *Gazette* carried a woodcut, drawn by Franklin, which portrayed a jointed snake, the joints not quite together, segments named for the colonies. "Join or die," read the caption.

The meaning was inescapable.

For three years Franklin had been advocating what Penn had urged years earlier. But the reactions of the various colonies had been desultory to say the least. The reason for that lack of enthusiasm was a feeling of well-being and self-confidence, particularly in the New England colonies. The fact was that the colonies regarded themselves as self-governing republics. Forget for a moment how Parliament regarded them. The people in Rhode Island and Connecticut, for example, were at this point well satisfied with their existence. They had been cut off by geographical circumstances from territorial ambition, and they had found solace in concentration of industrial development of a sort. So, when it came to considering expansion to the west, these colonies, Massachusetts to a degree, Georgia, Maryland, and Delaware really did not share the interest of such states as New York, Pennsylvania, and Virginia.

Franklin fretted for a few days, but then came an opportunity that he grasped as a chance to promote his idea at a time when all the colonies would be at least talking about the French depredations in the west.

The joint colonial board of trade, a voluntary organization for the promotion of intercolonial business, called a meeting at Albany of commissioners from several of the colonies to renew the trade and peace treaty with the Six Nations of Indians whose lands abutted their own.

Franklin secured the appointment as Pennsylvania commissioner. He was much pleased with this because it would give him a chance to further his greater plan.

There was no time to foment in Pennsylvania the sort of popular appeal that would lead to an assembly resolution or a show of popular backing for his position.

That position was already established. In 1751 a New Yorker, Archibald Kennedy, had proposed an intercolonial confederacy to work for common defense. That was all there was to Kennedy's proposal, but when he showed it to Franklin, it had sparked in Franklin the concept of a true intercolonial government, a federation to handle such matters as the common defense.

The idea had come to nothing, for in discussion of it he

had seen the difficulty of forming a union that would not in any way impinge upon the freedoms of the various colonies.

That point was paramount. Liberty to the colonists was the sort of watchword that could always rouse a sleeping man in a tavern to argue or fight. Liberty meant the right of men to conduct their business as they wished, to rise or fall on their merits without interference from anyone.

In this sense the colonists were a feisty lot. They valued liberty so highly that they were immediately suspicious of any plan that might deprive each colony of its own freedom of action, no matter how much it might promise in other ways.

Early in June, Franklin set out for Albany hoping that this time the greater threat of French and Indian pugnaciousness would persuade his other colonial friends that their common interest must overcome their individual desires. He now knew that men must be persuaded to give up a share of their liberty in favor of common defense. The observations of Locke about the nature of freedom were proving quite correct.

On June 19 the commissioners met at Albany. Franklin was there for Pennsylvania. All New England had sent men and so had Maryland.

Franklin was persuasive, and besides that, these men were quickly acquainted with the real dangers of French penetration. So on June 24 they agreed that a union of the colonies was absolutely essential for their preservation from the French.

Franklin, Thomas Hutchinson of Massachusetts, and a member from each of the other colonies met, and in four days drew up such a plan. Franklin, of course, had just happened to have a prototype in his pocket.

First of all, the Franklin plan called for preservation of the rights of the crown. Then the rights of the colonies must be preserved. But under that, the plan called for a general government to care for Indian affairs, common defense, and expansion of the colonies across the continent.

This government would have power to pass laws and to levy taxes.

The commissioners settled their affairs with the Indians and headed back, each to his own colony. In time every colony considered the plan and every colony rejected it. Even Pennsylvania looked askance at the possible curtailment of its liberties under such a union. As for England's feelings, the plan never officially arrived at all, and when news of it came, it was regarded as simply another colonial oddity.

That winter, not yet giving up hope, Franklin traveled to Boston on other business and there he conferred with Governor William Shirley. Shirley suggested a federative union in which the colonies would join the mother country as a unit and be represented in Parliament as Englishmen should—just as other regions of England were represented.

Franklin endorsed the idea warmly. He could see how such a union would make the English in Parliament understand American desires and needs. And he could see such a grand union making of the Empire "one community with one interest."

Perhaps, in spite of all the difficulties, something might have come of such schemes. Franklin's enthusiasm was remarkable, and when aroused he was a hard man to stop. Governor Shirley's alliance was an element that brought power and influence behind such planning; it would certainly be heard respectfully in London.

But the French and Indian wars intervened. The energies of all those concerned were taken up with immediate problems that quite precluded considerations of politics. It was in a way comparable to the forming of the United Nations in World War II.

The allies against the Rome-Berlin-Tokyo axis called themselves "United Nations" in the early 1940s, but it was not until the end of World War II that they were able to even consider the politics of such union.

So it was with the union Benjamin Franklin envisaged in the 1750s. By 1760, when France surrendered Canada and gave up her attempt to struggle for American colonies, the idea of union had been put very far back on the colonial agenda. And with no further common enemy to unite them, they scarcely considered it at all.

18

The Gadfly of Boston

It would be extreme to say that "if there had been no So and So there would have been no American Revolution" and, yet, the most cantankerous, stubborn, and opportunistic of all the colonial politicians seems to deserve that accolade in a way.

Samuel Adams, member of one of America's most distinguished families, was a propagandist and gossip but above all, a revolutionary.

He was born in 1722 and had the good fortune to attend Harvard College because his father was a prosperous merchant who also ran a brewery. The Adamses were immersed in public affairs; Sam's father was a deacon in the church, bank director, and backstairs politician. One of his little campaigns was against British impressment of New England seamen, which he called a breach of every basic law known to Massachusetts, the Magna Carta, the

British Constitution, and the charter of the province. The Deacon, as he was called, was a member of the Boston Caucus, a political club of shopkeepers and even working men, which controlled the selection of town officials.

The Adamses began really to hate the crown and all it stood for when their ox was gored in the early 1740s. Deacon Adams had gotten involved in a family inflationary he called the Land Bank, which issued paper money backed by real estate. Governor Jonathan Belcher outlawed the land bank, dismissed Deacon Adams as a justice of the peace, and thus earned the family's wrath. The Adamses were an unforgiving lot and Sam, then at Harvard College, saw his father's entire fortune threatened by the government's insistence that the directors of the bank pay off all its obligations. For twenty years Massachusetts tried to seize the deacon's estate.

Young Sam Adams became a merchant and brewer like his father, but he was bitten by the political bug and never much cared for making money. He was, as his friends were quick to discover, an expert at "viewing with alarm." He was an announced Puritan, and not a very pleasant fellow, and a dreadfully inept businessman. By 1758 he had made so many business mistakes that all that remained of the family fortune was the house and a brewery on Purchase Street.

Sam Adams' most vigorous enemy was Thomas Hutchinson, governor of the province who, with his father, had brought about the ruin of the Adamses, or so they believed, and there is nothing like personal animosity to feed a political grudge. By 1757 Adams was broke, with a wife and two small children, and was eking out his existence as a tax collector, and practicing radicalism.

His first major quarrel with London came in 1764 when Parliament passed the Sugar Act. This law laid a tax on sugar for the announced purpose of raising money

93

to support an army that would defend the American colonies. Previously, Parliament had considered the defense of America a part of the general expense of the Empire, but the heavy cost of the French and Indian wars had caused George III and his ministers to take a different view.

Adams, viewing with alarm as usual, saw in the tax on molasses (which the New Englanders used to make rum for trade) as the beginning of a trend. If Parliament could tax molasses, he said, then why would not Parliament tax everything else that belonged to the colonists, including their lands and houses?

The Massachusetts House of Representatives passed a resolution petitioning Parliament to repeal the Sugar Act, but Adams' plaints were really not given much importance.

From London's point of view, the colonies would become a liability if nothing was done. Having rejected Benjamin Franklin's proposal for a continental union, the colonies also squirmed and held back on any attempts to force them to pay for their own defense.

England was staggering under the immense debt incurred in the Seven Years' War, and British taxpayers in London grumbled so loudly about paying for the defense of the colonies that Parliament grew concerned and heeded the complaint in England. Englishmen simply balked at paying for defense of colonies they would never see.

With that rebellion at home, Parliament looked about for other means of protecting the national investment in America and the West Indies. And they found a source of income that had never been touched by direct taxation: the colonies themselves.

From the governors, from English travelers, and from the bankers of London, Parliament learned how rich the colonists had become during the Seven Years' War and the resentments mounted. This was all the more true because England began to convince herself that the only reason for the war against France had been the defense of the colonies, and so why should the colonies not bear that expense? Those rich rascals in America had been getting away with pleading poverty for too long; in London the rumor was that all Americans were rich.

And so George Grenville, Chancellor of the Exchequer, proposed that England should levy a series of revenue-raising measures on the colonists.

Along with the Sugar Act, Grenville in 1764 had placed new taxes on non-British textiles, on coffee and indigo, and on Madeira and Canary wine (which Englishmen were inclined to drink in quantities that would alarm a teetotaler). The Parliament doubled the duties on goods reshipped in England from foreign lands to the colonies. It added to the list of taxable items iron, hides, whale fins, raw silk, potash, and pearl ash. It banned the importation into the colonies of foreign rum and French wines.

At the same time London also indicated that it was really going to enforce these laws, and that was something else again.

Grenville, the politician, was interested in cementing power at home, and he recognized the reluctance of Englishmen to continue to bear the cost of the Empire. And so he suggested a tax on the colonials: a levy on newspapers, legal documents, and commercial papers.

From the English point of view it seemed an admirable solution. Nearly everyone at home agreed that the Americans should pay for their own defense. The Stamp Tax was a simple way. It was not particularly onerous. It was easy to collect, and it fell on the colonies in proportion to their wealth. In fact, for its time it was one of the fairest and most reasonable levies ever proposed.

Not only that, but it was not levied in haste. Grenville

proposed it and gracefully offered the colonies a year's time in which to come up with a better method of paying for defense.

The colonies had no intention of paying for anything if they could get out of it. So they let the year pass without offering anything at all. The miscalculation of Grenville was in regarding the American colonies as a unit. Had he studied the difficulties of Penn and Franklin in trying to achieve unity, he would have seen that there was precious little unity among these Americans, except in their unanimous pusillanimity when it came to anything regarding taxation.

Pusillanimity and pugnaciousness combined, that summed it up.

So when the year passed and there were no counteroffers, Parliament enacted the Stamp Tax, serene in the belief that Grenville had found the ideal, painless way to make the colonists contribute to their own defense.

London, then, was completely taken aback with the colonial response. The Americans behaved like teenagers of the 1970s told that they must cut their hair. They burned Grenville in effigy and they threatened Parliament. They were unified in this as in nothing else. For while the French and the Indians had seemingly threatened only some of the colonies, the tax would fall on everyone. London was the greater enemy that caused Americans to submerge their difficulties.

One could make a case then that England had been too lenient too long with these wayward children in the far country.

The reaction in America centered in groups that eventually united, more or less, under the banner of Sons of Liberty. For the most part these groups consisted of middle-class and artisan colonists who resented the privileges of the upper class that dominated colonial society.

In Boston, Samuel Adams was the fomenter, and most of his Sons of Liberty were working men of North Boston, the same unpropertied lot that had backed old Dean Adams in the Land Bank inflation scheme. The controlling mechanism was a committee that met in a counting room on the second floor of a distillery, in Hanover Square, near the Tree of Liberty, that great oak that had been planted three years before the beheading of Charles I.

Boston then came under the influence of what would be called a "trained mob" and Samuel Adams was its leader.

Actually, the alarm was sounded in Virginia where Patrick Henry caused the House of Burgesses to adopt the Virginia Resolves, with cries about liberty, death, and no taxation without representation.

But Massachusetts was not far behind and instead of "resolving" and converting fury to outraged words, the Boston mob began to act.

First came the sense of outrage. Times were hard in Boston in that year of 1765, and creditors were squeezing hard to get their money out of their debtors. It never occurred to the debtors that the burden of the Stamp Tax would fall on the possessors of wealth. The debtors rose up in a body to pull the creditors' chestnuts out of the fire.

Samuel Adams saw in this situation a chance to solve his own problem.

Having run through his family fortune, Adams had, as noted, supported himself in recent years as tax collector for Boston and the County of Suffolk. But he had in no way changed his ways; he was as careless with money as before. He began using his tax collections to support himself. For a few years he was able to conceal this by apparent slowness. He paid the treasuries very late and used this year's collections in part to satisfy last year's

97

taxes. But in 1764 it all caught up with him, and a little investigation showed that he was at least seven thousand pounds short in his accounts.

There was no getting around it. Sam Adams had been embezzling Boston's money, and it seemed certain he was bound for jail.

What better solution could there be than to overthrow the system that was about to destroy him? Or, to put it less trenchantly, Samuel Adams by this point had no cause to cherish the government under which he lived.

In the Summer of 1765 Adams led the mob in a series of terrorist actions. It began with the hanging, in effigy, from the Liberty Tree, of Andre Oliver, the Stamp Master of Massachusetts Bay.

On the morning of August 15, Bostonians came by the tree and saw the stuffed figure hanging.

That was only the beginning.

That night the mob, gathering strength as it went, paraded by the Town House where the governor and his council were in meeting, cheering and shouting noisily so the authorities would know they were out there. They marched to the waterfront, burned a building that was said to be the stamp headquarters, took the effigy to Oliver's house, and outside noisily beheaded it, with many baleful looks and loud shouts at the doorway.

At Fort Hill, the mob built a huge bonfire; then, fortified with rum and high spirits of hysteria, the mobsters decided they would really kill Oliver. They moved back to his house, broke the windows, forced their way in, and threatened all the while to kill him when they found him. But find him they did not, for he had left the city, or at least left his own house that day.

Next day he resigned as Stamp Master.

Samuel Adams saw that he had won a great victory,

98

and he determined to turn it against the Massachusetts government, whose justice hung so heavily over his head.

Within two weeks, by propaganda and word of mouth, he had fomented another riot. This time the rum-soaked mob broke into Lieutenant Governor Hutchinson's house, gutted it, destroyed his furniture, drank all the liquor and wines in his cellar, and tried to find him so they could murder him.

Next morning, fearful lest Hutchinson be regarded as a martyr, Samuel Adams announced that he, Hutchinson, was responsible for the Stamp Act. Adams knew it was a lie, but he did not care. He was not interested in truth, but in revolution.

By this time the mob instincts of the working people of Boston had been thoroughly aroused. They were never far from the surface anyhow; for years gangs in North Boston had fought with gangs of South Boston.

Samuel Adams set about unifying the mobs. He brought together Alexander McIntosh, the leader of the South End, and the leaders of the North End. They feasted at a banquet called the Union Feast and pledged undying loyalty to one another in the cause of freedom.

Freedom from what?

The nearest British troops were two hundred miles from Boston. The government of Governor Bernard had been notable for its timidity in enforcement of the laws.

And Samuel Adams and the mob took over Boston.

The royal governor retired to his castle. The stamps were packed in the warehouse. The port was opened without stamps, and the power of government was in the hands of Massachusetts men, in the legislative body and in the offices.

In November, representatives of the various colonies met in New York in congress to make a united protest to London against the Stamp Act. It was Adams' suggestion, made to James Otis, the Whig leader of the legislature. Otis' motion was adopted and sent to all the British colonies on the continent.

The congress did appeal to London. And when the representatives came back to Boston to report to the people, the rebellious Bostonians were well pleased.

"Who," demanded one of the patriots, "dreamt this time twelve months, of such a UNION of the colonies?"

19

The Way to Philadelphia

About a year before the controversy over the Stamp Act threw Boston into turmoil and affected men and women in every American colony, Stephen Hopkins, an important political figure in Rhode Island, wrote a pamphlet called, *The Rights of the Colonies Examined.*

He noted that all colonies had always enjoyed as much freedom "as the mother state," and so, obviously, should the American colonies of England.

He did not really define the rights of the colonies but he raised important questions about them. Did not the Americans have rights, and were they not to be the same rights that Englishmen had at home?

Even Thomas Hutchinson, who would later leave America because of his loyalty to the crown, said much the same in letters to friends in England.

And after the Stamp Act had brought the violence of

resistance to the colonies, the colonists felt it all the more important to justify their behavior. They did so by saying Parliament had no right to tax them as it was doing. Thus they arrived at a definition of colonial rights which was far broader than anything had been up to this time.

It was accepted at home in England that no Englishman could be taxed by government except by his own consent—that is, by his representatives in Parliament. And by extension, that right came across the Atlantic. Since Americans were not represented in Parliament, the home government had no right to tax them.

That discussion spread throughout the colonies quickly enough. Some suggested that it would not be hard to persuade Parliament to accept American representation. The more ardent slid over that quickly. They did not really want to be represented in Parliament; they wanted to be left alone.

Their contention was that Parliament could pass laws governing their conduct, but it could not pass "internal" measures such as the Stamp Act.

Parliament responded by passing the Townshend Acts, which, to honor the colonists, it declared were not "internal" taxes but "external," in regulation of trade.

It took some fancy footwork to find a method of legalizing opposition to these laws. John Dickinson, writing *Letters from a Farmer in Pennsylvania,* did so, however, with the tortured reasoning that went like this:

Parliament had the right to regulate trade, but not the right to levy taxes on America without consent. What was the purpose of the Townshend Acts? Why, it was to raise revenue as well as regulate trade, and so it was a tax, and therefore illegal.

And by 1770 Benjamin Franklin had come to one final conclusion about the whole matter of legislation. Either Parliament had the power of making all laws for the colonies, or it had no power to make any laws for them. Which was it to be? Thus developed the theory that all parts of the British Empire should be subject to the king, but that each part should have its own legislature.

At that time James Wilson was writing a pamphlet, *Considerations on the Nature and Extent of the Legislative Authority of the British Parliament,* which said the same thing.

And he wrote:

"All men are, by nature, equal and free. No one has a right to any authority over another without his consent. All lawful government is founded in the consent of those who are subject to it. Such consent is given with a view to insure and to increase the happiness of the governed above what they would enjoy in an independent and unconnected state of nature. The consequence is that the happiness of the society is the first law of every government."

That writing was stuffed away in Wilson's desk shortly afterward and half forgotten by this busy lawyer, for it seemed that the difficulties between the colonies and Parliament were going to be resolved sensibly.

But then, in 1773, Parliament gave the East India Company a monopoly of the American tea trade. When the tea came, with a tax, the Americans dumped a cargo of it into Boston Harbor.

The East India Company's owners were furious. They aroused Parliament, and that body passed the Coercive Acts to teach Massachusetts a lesson that included closing the port, provided for the movement of court cases to London, and called for quartering British troops in the recalcitrant town.

The colonies responded by calling a congress of deputies to Philadelphia on September 5, 1774.

The purpose of this congress was to convince the people of Britain that the Americans were in dead earnest about their rights and determined to defend them.

But the delegates first of all had to agree on what those rights were.

They talked and argued and discussed the matter, and finally John Adams of Boston was asked to put something down on paper.

He wrote the Declaration of Rights.

Americans, it said, were entitled to life, liberty, and property. They also merited the rights, liberties, and immunities of free and natural-born subjects within the realm of England.

Further, said Adams, the foundation of English liberty was the right to participate in legislative council. Since the Americans were too far away to be properly represented in Parliament, then legislation over their affairs could only be passed by the various colonial legislatures, in cases of taxation and internal policy, subject only to the veto of the king.

Aside from this, said Adams, "We cheerfully consent to the operation of such acts of the British Parliament as are bona fide."

And this was the position adopted by the colonies all through 1774 and 1775, even after the war broke out. The war was not being fought in '75 for independence. It was waged to defy British misrule and to force Parliament into accepting the American point of view about its legislative authority.

Indeed, Dickinson prepared a petition to the king, stating that to be the case.

"We have not raised armies with ambitious designs of separating from Great Britain . . ." it said. "We shall lay them down when hostilities shall cease on the part of the aggressors. . . ."

But the king refused to accept the petition, and the government in London issued the Prohibitory Act of December 22, 1775, which declared the colonies in insurrection and ordered a blockade of all their ports.

The fact was that most Americans did not want independence from England.

But at the same time they were determined not to submit to Parliament's rule over them. And so in the Winter of early 1776, the colonists reluctantly began to realize that they either had to submit or carry on alone, forever.

"We are between hawk and buzzard," said Robert Livingston.

And the others agreed. What they needed by that time were supplies to continue the war and meet the needs of the people. Britain had cut off her trade with the colonies, and it was hurting badly.

They could turn to France, of course, because the French were Britain's enemies and would like to hurt her if they could. But if they turned to France they had to have a new entity. They could not say to the French, "We are Englishmen who are having a quarrel with the mother country and want your help."

They would have to say, "We are free men who need your help."

That decision was made in the Spring of 1776, and the ports of America were opened by Congress to the trade of the world, in direct violation of all practice and law of Britain.

With that action in April, the Declaration of Independence became inevitable.

20

Washington, the Catalyst

After the struggle began with the firing at Lexington and Concord, the colonial armies assembled around Boston, and George Washington was soon placed in command by Congress, as the most experienced officer from one of the largest colonies.

That Summer, Fall, and Winter of 1775, Washington had been facing the British around Boston. Because of severe losses and the temper of the inhabitants, the British were cautious about attacking again in the interior of New England.

But in January 1776, half the enlistments of Washington's troops expired, and the men began going home. Why stay? What was there to hold a Virginian or a Jerseyman, or a Carolinian up here in the cold north when he could be back home getting ready to put in the crops?

The war seemed almost over, and what were they fighting about? The issues that had seemed so clear in Massachusetts in the spring now seemed confused and the leadership befuddled.

So the soldiers began drifting away, summer soldiers at heart, with no common cause to join them into a fighting army.

Washington could see that if affairs continued in this manner the colonies would be forced to submit to England's yoke because there would be no military force to oppose the redcoats and their Hessian hirelings.

It was then in the Winter and Spring of 1775–1776 that Washington began to implore Congress for aid. He needed material supplies, but far more he needed political decision and firm action; let Congress do something about the war in terms of making it a definitive contest rather than an attempt to get better terms by half the colonies, as it had begun.

Congress began to debate. Many delegates in Philadelphia were decidedly lukewarm about Washington's suggestion. It was one thing to rise up against the tyranny of the crown's governors, but it was quite something else to take the final step of TREASON against the crown.

And yet, as Congress could see from the letters, the war would not wait. In March 1776, Washington shifted his army from Boston to New York, anticipating General Howe's plan to use New York as his base of operations. The situation was growing desperate.

21

The Assemblage

One factor in the opening of the ports to foreigners in the Spring of 1776 was the violent action of Lord Dunmore, Royal Governor of Virginia, who left his palace in Williamsburg and took refuge aboard a British warship when the colonies began to erupt. From there he called on Negro slaves to rebel against the colonists and join the loyal forces of the king. He also caused the bombardment of the port of Norfolk, which led to a dreadful fire that destroyed much of the town.

Another factor was a forty-seven-page pamphlet, published in January of 1776, called *Common Sense,* the creation of a thirty-nine-year-old journalist named Thomas Paine.

Many people in the colonies thought Ben Franklin had written the pamphlet. The style was much like his, it seemed to them, and Franklin was not above a sly anonymous gesture of this sort.

Nearly all of what Paine said about the issues dividing Americans from Britons had been said before by others, but no one had put it all together in such a clarion call for independence from Britain. "A government of our own is a natural right," he declared.

Soon the pamphlet was in its second printing, then its third, and more. In the first three months, one hundred and twenty thousand copies were sold. It spread like wildfire across the colonies and magnified its appeal as it went.

And so, on April 12, the Provincial Congress of North Carolina instructed its delegates to the Congress that would be reassembling in Philadelphia next month to support "independency" for Americans.

Another center of the storm was Virginia, where Patrick Henry and Peyton Randolph were thundering in favor of liberty from England. The people there, too, were reading and talking about *Common Sense*.

On that same day that North Carolina passed its resolution, traveler John Page wrote a friend:

"In my way through Virginia, I found the inhabitants warm for independence. . . . Indeed I hear nothing praised but *Common Sense* and Independence. . . ."

In Philadelphia, John Adams was annoyed by Paine's work, not so much because he did not agree with it, but because Paine was becoming famous for it and Adams, who had a low level of toleration, was jealous of the other. But even Adams wrote his wife that the country was seized by the pamphlet as it had not been by any other work, and everywhere men were talking of the ringing words:

". . . Let the names of whig and tory be extinct; and let none other be heard among us than those of a good citizen, an open and resolute friend, and a virtuous sup-

109

porter of the Rights of Mankind, and of the Free and Independent States of America. . . ."

By early May Congress, in Philadelphia, had adopted a resolution calling on the various colonies to form governments of their own. The debate on this issue had been heated, for the New Englanders and the Southerners were pressing for independence; the men of the middle colonies were not so certain about it.

And then, on May 27, the resolution from North Carolina arrived, as did the one from Virginia, saying much the same thing.

On June 7 Richard Henry Lee made a formal proposal to Congress that summed up all the feelings of the militants:

"That these United Colonies are, and of right ought to be, free and independent States, that they are absolved from all allegiance to the British Crown, and that all political connection between them and the State of Great Britain is, and ought to be, totally dissolved.

"That it is expedient forthwith to take the most effectual measures for forming foreign alliances.

"That a plan of confederation be prepared and transmitted to the respective Colonies for their consideration and approbation."

Thus spoke the senior member of the Virginia delegation, and the motion was seconded by John Adams. They carried the debate, aided by George Wythe of Virginia, an eloquent orator. Thomas Jefferson, who hated public speaking, sat quietly and kept notes.

There was a spirited debate, because the Pennsylvania, New York, and South Carolina delegates were not at all sure they were ready to go so far so fast.

Since public meetings had been called in the middle states, the delegates to Congress agreed to postpone the

110

discussion of the motion a few weeks until the meetings had been held.

But since the sentiment in Congress was so strong for independence, Congress named a committee to draw up a paper in the interim. The committee consisted of John Adams, Thomas Jefferson, Benjamin Franklin, Roger Sherman, and Robert R. Livingston.

As they worked, the word came that Virginia was moving already. Soon Virginia would call herself a state and would elect her own governor, Patrick Henry, to replace Governor Dunmore.

That breach was final.

22

Drafting the Declaration

The committee was appointed on June 11, 1776, to prepare a Declaration of Independence, and it promptly met to select a subcommittee.

First the five discussed the articles that would be contained in the declaration. Agreed upon these, they then named Adams and Jefferson to make the actual draft.

The subcommittee of two then met, and Jefferson suggested that Adams do the drafting.

"I will not," said Adams.

"You shall do it," said Jefferson.

"Oh no!"

"Why will you not?"

"Reasons enough."

"What can be your reasons?"

Adams ticked them off:

"First Reason: You are a Virginian and a Virginian

ought to appear at the head of this business. Reason second, I am obnoxious, suspected and unpopular; you are very much otherwise. Reason third, you can write ten times better than I can."

"Well," said Jefferson, "if you are decided I will do as well as I can."

"Very well, when you have drawn it up we will have a meeting."

That was Adams' recollection of the events. Jefferson's was different, but the essence was really the same: Jefferson was selected to draft the declaration.

Adams' remarks about Jefferson were certainly true enough. The resolution for independence had been introduced in Virginia's name, Virginia had been in the forefront of colonial enterprise and protest against the crown since the Stamp Act. And as for Jefferson, although he was only thirty-three, he was well-known in the colonies as a literary fellow and scientist.

Jefferson then went back to his lodgings in the house of a man named Graff at the southwest corner of Seventh and Market streets. It was a three-story brick house and Jefferson had the whole second floor to himself, divided into a parlor and a bedroom.

In the parlor was Jefferson's portable writing desk, an invention of his own, which had been made for him by a cabinetmaker in Philadelphia. The writing desk had already been put to hard use that spring. At this same desk Jefferson had drafted a constitution for Virginia, which he had sent down to Williamsburg with his old teacher George Wythe, when he went home to attend that convention.

So Jefferson had been thinking a good deal about the elements of the declaration. He had begun the draft of the constitution with a preamble that attacked George III for establishing tyranny over America. Now he sat down in the rented parlor to improve on his handiwork.

Jefferson did not have his library available to him in Philadelphia, but he scarcely needed it. Under Wythe in Williamsburg he had studied John Locke, he had read virtually all the works published in Europe on the subject of natural law and the rights of men since the days of the Glorious Revolution, and even before. He had long been pondering the relations between the colonies and the mother country, and like many another, he had come to firm conclusions as strong as those expressed by Thomas Paine.

He was particularly full of thoughts about the charges to be levied against King George III, because it was essential to the purposes of the colonists that they prove how they had been mistreated by this king, to the point that dissolution of bonds was the only remaining answer.

Earlier, in Virginia, Jefferson's associates had produced a Declaration of Rights, proclaiming many of the liberties they had all discussed, and this document had just appeared in Philadelphia recently.

In his parlor in Philadelphia, then, Jefferson took up pen and ink and sat down in a chair, his portable desk across his knee, and began to write.

He considered the sins of George III:

"He has refused his assent to laws . . . dissolved the Representative Houses . . . combined with others to subject us to a jurisdiction foreign to our constitution . . . plundered our seas, ravaged our coasts, burnt our towns, and destroyed the lives of our people . . . his . . . transporting large armies of foreign mercenaries to complete the works of death, desolation, and tyranny already begun with circumstances of cruelty and perfidy . . . he has endeavored to bring on the inhabitants of our frontiers the merciless Indian savages. . . ."

114

Indictment after indictment came tumbling forth as Jefferson wrote page upon page of the detail of George III's crimes against America.

Finally, the document was drafted. He showed it first of all to John Adams and to Benjamin Franklin.

They had some ideas of their own.

Franklin suggested a change in the section that had discussed the administration of justice. Where Jefferson had said George III had done wrong by making judges dependent on him alone for tenure and amount of their salaries, the practical Franklin said it ought to read "the" amount "and payment" of their salaries.

There were a few other suggested changes, and Jefferson incorporated them all. Then he showed the draft to Adams, who had some changes of his own, based largely on the experience of Massachusetts, which had fallen early under the heel of George III and suffered sorely.

Once this was done, Jefferson took the draft back, made some revisions to sharpen the language and improve his phrasing, and then apparently showed it once more to his two associates for more changes.

By this time there were some sixteen changes in his draft, plus three new paragraphs he had seen fit to write. And this copy, then, seems to have been submitted to the committee of five. Franklin and Adams had copies of the draft for themselves, and Jefferson had a rough draft and a copy.

All of this occurred during the next to last week of June.

On June 28 the committee of five announced that it was ready to report.

23

Virginia Leads the Way

As everyone knew, the Virginia convention of May 1776 was going to be the most important in the history of the colony. All through the colony local bodies were meeting, talking of Thomas Paine's *Common Sense* and declaring for independence.

Cumberland, for example, held its county meeting on April 22 and announced that "we . . . your constituents, instruct you positively to declare for an independency, that you solemnly abjure any allegiance to his Brittanick majesty and bid him a goodnight forever. . . ." A day later, Charlotte County instructed its delegates to be sure that the people sent to Congress "cast off the British yoke. . . ."

And so when the Virginians met in Williamsburg on May 15, they got right down to business.

". . . Resolved unanimously, that the Delegates ap-

116

pointed to represent this colony in General Congress be instructed to propose to that respectable body to declare the United Colonies free and independent states. . . ."

The next day, after the briefest of sessions, the convention shut its doors and joined in the general rejoicing of the populace.

On the seventeenth, *Purdie's Gazette* dropped from its masthead the royal coat of arms and motto, *En dat Virginia quartam,* and substituted for it a new slogan:

THIRTEEN UNITED COLONIES
"United we stand——Divided, we fall."

That day the Convention was back at work, the merrymaking and celebration having given way to sober thoughts. The task ahead was enormous, and these men in Williamsburg were well aware of the ramifications of what they had done; the Lord knew they had discussed all those ramifications enough times in recent months.

In attendance at Williamsburg this day was George Mason, Virginia gentleman, constitutional student, and now a statesman, whose hand would shape the destiny of his state and the nation far more firmly than many would ever know.

Mason and Thomas Jefferson were the leaders of the Virginia moderates, the glue that held together the backwoodsmen of the West and the aristocrats of tidewater country.

Mason came to Williamsburg on May 17 and was immediately appointed to the committee assigned the task of writing a declaration of rights and a constitution for the new government. Having abjured the old, they must create the new.

The committee worked for a week and then came forth

117

with a draft of a document declaring the rights of Virginians.

Mason was the principal author of this work, and for it he drew on knowledge that dipped far back into the English past. The reference to Locke's *Treatise of Civil Government* was obvious, and his idea of the reservation of powers to the individual. But much else came from disparate sources, and some from experiences that Mason had known in Virginia, in matters affecting newspapers (suppressed) and religion (harried) under the royal governors of the colony.

Here is how the first draft began; after the titling:

1. That all men are created equally free and independent, and have certain inherent natural rights, of which they cannot by any compact, deprive or divest their posterity; among which are the enjoyment of life and liberty, with the means of acquiring and possessing property, and pursuing and obtaining happiness and safety.

2. That all power is by God and Nature vested in, and consequently derived from, the people; that the magistrates are their trustees and servants, and at all times amenable to them.

3. That government is, or ought to be, instituted for the common benefit, protection and security of the people, nation, or community. Of all the various modes and forms of government that is best which is capable of producing the greatest degree of happiness and safety, and is most effectively secured against the dangers of mal-administration; and that whenever any government shall be found inadequate or contrary to these purposes, a majority of the community hath an indubitable, unalienable, and indefeasible right to reform, alter, or abolish it, in such a manner as shall be judged most conducive to the public weal.

4. That no man, or set of men, are entitled to exclusive or separate emoluments or privileges from the community,

118

but in consideration of public services, which not being descendible, neither ought the offices of magistrate, legislator, or judge to be hereditary.

5. That the legislative and executive powers of the State should be separate and as distinct from the judicial; and that the members of the two first may be restrained from oppression by feeling and participating the burdens of the people. They should, at fixed periods, be reduced to a private station, and return to that body from which they were originally taken, and the vacancies be supplied by frequent, certain, and regular elections.

6. That elections of members to serve as representatives of the people in the legislature ought to be free, and that all men, having sufficient evidence of permanent, common interest with, and attachment to, the community, have the right of suffrage and cannot be taxed or deprived of their property for public uses, without their own consent, or that of their representatives, so elected, nor found by any law to which they have not, in like manner, assented for the common good.

7. That all power of suspending laws, or the execution of laws, by any authority, without consent of the representatives of the people, is injurious to their rights, and ought not be exercised.

8. That in all capital or criminal prosecutions a man has a right to demand the cause and nature of his accusation, to be confronted with the accusers and witnesses, to call for evidence in his favor, and to have a speedy trial by an impartial jury of his vicinage, without whose unanimous consent he cannot be found guilty, nor can he be compelled to give evidence against himself, and that no man be deprived of his liberty except by the law of the land or the judgment of his peers.

9. That excessive bail ought not to be required, nor ex-

cessive fines imposed, nor cruel and unusual punishments inflicted.

10. That in controversies respecting property, and in suits between man and man, the ancient trial by jury is preferable to any other, and to be held sacred.

11. That freedom of the press is one of the great bulwarks of liberty, and can never be restrained but by despotic governments.

12. That a well-regulated militia, composed of the body of the people, trained to arms, is the proper, natural, and safe defense of a free state; that standing armies in time of peace should be avoided, as dangerous to liberty, and that in all cases the military should be under strict subordination to, and governed by, the civil power.

13. That no free government, or the blessing of liberty, can be preserved to any people but by a firm adherence to justice, moderation, temperance, frugality, and virtue, and by frequent recurrence to fundamental principles.

14. That religion, or the duty which we owe our Creator, and the manner of discharging it, can be directed only by reason and conviction, not by force or violence, and therefore that all men should enjoy the fullest toleration in the exercise of religion, according to the dictates of Conscience, unpunished and restrained by the magistrates, unless, under color of religion, any man disturb the peace, the happiness, or the safety of society. And that it is the mutual duty of all to practice Christian forbearance, love, and charity towards each other.

Mason's Bill of Rights was debated for two weeks, and then on June 15 it was unanimously adopted, with few changes. So there was George Mason's magnum opus. It was hurried up to Philadelphia and a copy placed in the hands of Thomas Jefferson, who studied it carefully.

Then Jefferson began to write. . . .

24

Debate

The committee of five left the drafted declaration with Secretary Charles Thomson, and four days after they submitted it, Congress was ready to discuss the matter. The meetings had been held in New York and Pennsylvania, the once lukewarm delegates from South Carolina had become convinced, and Congress was ready to take an action that by now was certainly necessary if the war was to continue.

For the purposes of discussion of the declaration, Congress formed itself into a committee of the whole.

The debate began, and Jefferson, miserable in the arguments that developed over his language, sat and took notes on it.

John Adams spoke fervently in support of the document as written, but the other delegates of Congress were not going to be stampeded into approving something they had not considered fully.

Some of the delegates believed America still had many friends in England (a "pusillanimous idea," Jefferson called it) and so the whole section that dealt with "our British brethren" received a thorough overhaul. The most telling phrases were stricken, the reference to "Scotch & foreign mercenaries" was stricken, partly on grounds that Scotland could be friendly, partly because many a Scot had settled in America.

Then, too, Jefferson had devoted nearly two hundred words to a ringing indictment of the slave trade.

"He (George III) has waged cruel war against human nature itself, violating its most sacred rights of life and liberty in the persons of a distant people who never offended him, captivating and carrying them into slavery in another hemisphere, or to incur miserable death in their transportation thither. This piratical warfare, the opprobrium of infidel powers, is the warfare on the Christian King of Great Britain. Determined to keep open a market where MEN should be bought and sold, he has prostituted his negative for suppressing every legislative attempt to prohibit or to restrain this execrable commerce, and that this assemblage of horrors might want no fact of distinguished die, he is now exciting those very people to rise in arms among us, and to purchase that liberty of which he has deprived them, by murdering the people upon whom he also obtruded them; thus paying off former crimes committed against the liberties of one people with crimes which he urges them to commit against the lives of another. . . ."

The South Carolina and Georgia delegations had harsh words to say about this section of the Declaration. South Carolina had sent four delegates to Philadelphia. Arthur Middleton, at thirty-four, was the oldest. He was queasy about the whole enterprise, and why not? Son of one of the South's largest slaveholders, with a score of plantations and eight hundred blacks who "belonged" to the family, Middleton was educated largely in England, and his ties were strong.

Thomas Heyward, Jr., thirty at this time, was another member of the slaveholding aristocracy. He, too, had spent much time in London, and like Middleton he had read law at the Middle Temple there.

Edward Rutledge, twenty-six, was the youngest member of Congress, and his brief career had been almost a carbon copy of Middleton's and Heyward's. He had actually been more responsible than any other for the postponement of the entire independence matter during the month of June.

The fourth member of the South Carolina delegation was Thomas Lynch, Jr. Lynch had studied at Eton and Cambridge, and then the Middle Temple. But oddly enough, he, the most Anglicized of them all, was also the most radical of the South Carolinians on the subject of independence.

Even on July 2, when Congress convened to begin the discussions of the Declaration, the South Carolinians were not apparently certain of their position. They were committed but queasy.

The Georgians joined them, not on the issues of friendship with Britons, but on the slave trade matter.

One Georgian was Lyman Hall, fifty-two, a rice planter and physician whose home was near Savannah.

Button Gwinett, forty-one, was English and had an English wife, and he, too, was a planter on St. Catherine's Island off the coast.

George Walton, thirty-five, was the third member of the Georgia delegation and perhaps the most active patriot of them all.

The Georgia and South Carolina delegations spoke now against the strong language used to castigate the slave trade. The fact was that they had no fault to find with the trade. It brought them the workers they needed in their fields. Indeed, they felt it important that the trade be continued.

And some of the Northerners agreed, at least privately, for they and their friends and relatives had been involved in carrying slaves across the Atlantic very profitably.

Jefferson squirmed, then, as the whole section on which he felt so strongly was excised from his Declaration.

Sitting nearby, Benjamin Franklin saw his young friend's discomfiture and turned to him.

"I have made it a rule," said Franklin, "whenever in my power, to avoid becoming the draughtsman of papers to be reviewed by a public body."

And he told Jefferson a story.

When Franklin was a journeyman printer, one of his friends, an apprentice hatter, had served out his time and could establish himself as a journeyman in the trade. So as he was about to open shop, the young hatter decided the first thing he needed was a signboard, and he set about composing the inscription for it.

"John Thompson, Hatter, makes and sells hats for ready money," he wrote with a flourish, and was well pleased. There would be a drawing of a hat right next to the words. He then took his sign to friends to see what they thought about it.

The first friends pointed out that the word "hatter" was unnecessary, because it was followed by the words "makes hats." So that was struck out.

"John Thompson, makes and sells hats for ready money," said the sign, then, with its picture of the hat.

The second friend noted that he ought to take out the word "makes," because who cared who made the hats? If

124

they were good hats, everybody would want them no matter who had made them. So "makes" was struck out.

"John Thompson sells hats for ready money," the sign read.

The third friend pointed out that no one around that area sold anything on credit, so why would he need to belabor the obvious and say "for ready money."

A little grimly, John Thompson struck out "ready money."

"John Thompson sells hats" read the sign with the figure of the hat next to the words.

"Sells hats?" demanded his next friend. "Why nobody will expect you to give them away. What use is that word?" And so the word "sells" was stricken.

"John Thompson, hats" was the sign now. And his last friend pointed out the obvious: since he had a picture of a hat right next to his name, why in the world would he need the word "hats" at all.

So there it was, finally. John Thompson had his sign.

"John Thompson," and a picture of a hat.

So Congress debated, and made changes, and left out phrases, and added words here and there. And if it is often said that a committee cannot write a document, why then at least it must also be said that the Declaration of Independence as amended by Adams and Franklin and Congress in session was better for the changes than Jefferson's original; it was sharper, more cogent, simpler, and divorced from extravagances of language.

By this time a number of copies of the Declaration had been made, showing it in various stages of change. Adams had a copy, and so did Jefferson have at least one, and there must have been others for the committee of five.

Jefferson preserved one copy, which he called the rough draft, and later he sent one to Richard Henry Lee, which eventually found its way into the hands of the

125

American Philosophical Society, which printed it in facsimile in the Proceedings of the Society many years later.

The debate went on and on and on, and as John Adams said, ". . . nothing was said but what has been repeated and hackneyed in that room before a hundred times for six months past. . . ."

Finally, the question was called, as all concerned recognized the truth of Adams remarks.

Pennsylvania and South Carolina voted no. Delaware's delegates split down the middle, and New York abstained.

A majority of nine states had voted for independence, so the measure was passed in that sense. But, obviously, that was not good enough in such a matter; unanimity must be achieved at all costs.

That night, James Wilson of Pennsylvania undertook some politicking. He and Benjamin Franklin were for the Declaration, of course, but four others in the delegation were opposed. And yet something must be done. When Congress met on July 2, and the matter was brought up once more, two of the opponents did not take their seats, and so Wilson, Franklin, and John Morton carried the day against Thomas Willing and David Humphreys, who never gave in. South Carolina surrendered gracefully, and Delaware put on its best face and voted for independence since a missing member of the delegation had only just arrived to swing the vote. Only New York declined to be counted. The New York delegates said they had no instructions that would permit them to take such an act, and so they were silent.

It was, said John Adams, writing home to Boston, "the greatest question . . . which was ever debated in America, and a greater, perhaps never was nor will be decided among men. . . ."

On July 4, Benjamin Harrison reported that the committee of the whole Congress had agreed to the Declaration; then it was read. That rough copy of the Declaration may have been authenticated by the signatures of President John Hancock and Secretary Charles Thomson. But no one knows for sure because that copy did not survive. No one else was asked to sign it then.

It was ordered to be printed that night. John Dunlap was the printer selected, and the document immediately went to his printing shop. By early morning eighty to one hundred copies of the broadside, or poster, were printed.

A blank space had been left in the journal of the previous day, so on July 5 it was filled with Dunlap's Declaration and attached with wax. This, then, was the first official copy of the Declaration of Independence.

But it was not a unanimous document or agreement. For in the final vote, New York had abstained.

The Declaration had been enacted, however, by the members of Congress, and Congress ordered copies sent to the assemblies, the conventions, the committees of safety, the various units of American troops. The purpose was to have the decision, the document, the ringing declaration, shouted out in the land.

The various copies were dispatched from Philadelphia on July 5.

It all took a bit of time. Even in Philadelphia where the Declaration was received almost immediately by the Committee of Safety, it was not until July 8 that a celebration could be arranged and the Declaration promulgated, probably by John Nixon, a prominent member of the committee.

The celebrations continued throughout the colonies. On July 9 General Washington had the troops drawn up in New York, where he was, and heard it read.

That night, in New York, the equestrian statue of

George III was overturned. The people of New York had spoken, even if their representatives in Congress had not.

Boston did not get its Declaration until July 18, when the people gathered in front of the State House and heard the Declaration read, then cheered and went out to burn the king's coat of arms in King Street.

Perhaps the last place for the Declaration to arrive was the remote town of Savannah, where it came in the middle of August and was read at the Liberty pole while officials and gentlemen dined and drank toasts under the trees—toasts to Liberty, to Congress, to Georgia, to the victory of the armies—and not a one to old King George.

By July 19, word that New York had voted for the Declaration reached Congress. The decision was made that date to have the Declaration engrossed on parchment and signed by every member of Congress.

The copying, it is said, was done by Timothy Matlack of Philadelphia, who had been Charles Thomson's assistant secretary of Congress. It was done late in July, and on August 2 it was signed.

But it was not signed by all those who had actually passed on it, and it was signed by some who had not. And some signed later. Signing was declared a closed matter in 1781 five years after the document was first approved.

From this point on, the story becomes a tale of a literary history.

25

The Document

The "original" Declaration of Independence, the parchment document, is no such thing, of course, but designed to be a carefully drawn instrument that was to be saved for posterity. Jefferson's rough draft, which may have been signed by Hancock and Thomson, was probably used by the printer and then lost, but fragments of another draft survived.

But what was real? Jefferson drew a document. He worked it over for several days by himself and then was assisted by John Adams and Benjamin Franklin. The committee of five then worked on it, and finally the drafted document was read, discussed, and changed considerably by Congress. It was, for example, amended more than George Mason's Declaration of Rights for Virginians was changed by that new state's convention.

The printed copies were distributed. Only one was kept

in the journal of July 4 as a paper of Congress. The parchment copy of the Declaration was kept in the hands of Secretary Charles Thomson. When Congress became alarmed at the coming of the British in the fall of 1776 and moved quickly to Baltimore, the journal, the hand-written Declaration, and other papers were moved by wagon.

And in Baltimore, the Declaration was printed for the second time with the names of the signers attached.

Congress and the Declaration went back to Philadelphia in the Spring of 1777 when the British were gone. But they fled again, this time down to Lancaster and then to York. The Declaration was stored in the courthouse there.

It followed the fortunes of Congress, back to Philadelphia, and then to Princeton, Trenton, Annapolis, and New York City in 1785, as the seat of American government changed.

When the United States of America was established in 1789 and George Washington was inaugurated president, the Declaration of Independence was turned over to the secretary of state and remained in his custody. That meant New York City in the beginning, on lower Broadway in the offices of the secretary of state. In 1790, the government moved back to Philadelphia for ten years, and then to Washington, in the District of Columbia, the new Federal city.

The Declaration came down to the muddy city in 1800 and was stored in the War Office Building on Seventeenth Street.

In 1814 when the British burned Washington, Secretary of State James Monroe had enough advance warning of their descent on the city to pack up the state papers in linen sacks and cart them off to safety. The Declaration was stored in a barn near Chain Bridge and then in the house of a minister named Littlejohn in Leesburg, Virginia.

But Washington was soon enough recovered from the British, who were making a raid and not occupying, and the Declaration came back. In 1820 it was moved to the new offices of the State Department where the Treasury now stands.

By this time, copies of the Declaration had been made by a number of enterprising printers. A professional penman named Benjamin Owen Tyler brought out a copy of the Declaration that was really a forgery, in that he had imitated the signatures of the signers. But it was so good a job that many people did not even know it.

A more elaborate edition was brought out by John Binns, who sold many copies to the public. Various editions by the hundreds have been printed, especially during the first century and a half after 1776.

In 1823 Secretary of State John Quincy Adams had an exact facsimile of the Declaration made and sent copies to all the surviving signers. Much of the original ink was destroyed by the copper etching process approved by Adams. Other copies were given to high officials and some friends of the administration.

The Declaration was rolled up and stored away until 1841, when Secretary of State Daniel Webster had it moved to the new Patent Office Building, where it was framed and hung on the wall along with George Washington's commission as commander in chief of the forces of Congress.

It hung opposite a window and the bright light soon began yellowing the parchment. It was noticed by visitors and they talked about it, but nothing was done, and so in 1876 when it was taken to Philadelphia for the Centennial Exposition, the text was faded and many of the signatures had become either invisible or unrecognizable.

After Philadelphia, the Declaration came back to Washington and was hung for seventeen more years in the Department of State.

Many officials wondered at the condition of the document and there was talk about restoration. One proposal was advanced to retrace the writing, but it was not done.

But finally in 1894 Secretary of State Walter Q. Gresham decided the document should no longer be exhibited in the interest of preserving it. It was sealed between two plates of glass to keep it flat and locked in a safe, where it remained in the dark for the next twenty-five years.

In 1921, Secretary of State Charles Evans Hughes suggested that the Declaration be moved to the Library of Congress, and it was, along with the Constitution, to the office of Dr. Herbert Putnam, the librarian of Congress.

Congress appropriated money for a special area to be made to exhibit the documents, and they were shown there after the turn of 1924. They remained until Pearl Harbor, and the war against Japan and Germany, when they were taken to Fort Knox to protect them against possible enemy attack of some sort.

Some repair was done to the Declaration there. Cracks were drawn together and old glue taken off. Then on October 1, 1944, the two documents (the printed version and the handwritten version) were brought back and displayed again at the Library of Congress.

This being an age of science, tests were made and new ways sought to preserve the documents. They were sealed in insulating glass and in a vacuum, and temperature was carefully controlled.

Then in 1952 the documents were moved to the new National Archives building and once again put on permanent display, this time under controlled conditions that should last for many centuries.

26

The Auction

On December 31, 1968, Leary's Book Store in Philadelphia was preparing to go out of business after 132 years of selling to the public. The owners planned an auction and hired the firm of Samuel T. Freeman & Co. to undertake it.

In the course of checking the stock, the booksellers came upon some old wooden crates in a dark corner of the sixth floor of the building. They had been ignored for years because they were believed to contain printing plates from the nineteenth century when Leary's had been in the publishing business. In one of the crates the cataloguers came across a dusty copy of a broadside of the Declaration of Independence.

Philadelphia . . . old book store . . . Declaration of Independence. . . .

The thoughts connected rapidly. Was there a chance,

could it be, a rare, hitherto unknown copy of the original printing of the Declaration of Independence?

After the Congress had voted to make the Declaration official, on July 4, the final document with many changes made had been delivered to John Dunlap, the official printer of Congress, in his shop at High and Market streets.

That night the type was set and the Declaration printed in broadside as ordered by Congress so it could send copies across the land.

Some eighty to one hundred copies were printed, historians believe. Next day, and thereafter, Congress began dispatching them to Boston, to Williamsburg, to the capitals, and to the armies, so that the word would be spread.

Most copies reached their destination and were then often used to print new broadsides so that all America might know.

One copy fell into the hands of General William Howe and Admiral Richard Howe not long after it was dispatched from Philadelphia, and they sent it on to London. And then the copies of the printed Declaration began to scatter.

Over the years most were lost. Some were presented to various institutions, such as the American Philosophical Society in Philadelphia, and some found their way into the hands of families.

By 1969 all known copies were in the hands of public institutions, and these numbered only seventeen. By 1976 the number had grown to twenty-one. Several in private hands had come to light. Three are copies with roughly half missing.

The booksellers took their find to the American Philosophical Society where several experts verified the copy as off the same printing as their own Dunlap copy. To be absolutely certain they asked Frederick R. Goff, Chief of the Rare Book Division of the Library of Congress, to come to Philadelphia. He confirmed in writing the authenticity of the document.

The news was out, and within a matter of hours it was printed by newspapers throughout the country.

I read an article in *The New York Times* about the discovery of the printed copy at Leary's Book Store. I was aware that a copy of the Constitution had been auctioned several weeks earlier for approximately $200,000. I estimated as a result that the Declaration of Independence would go for about $325,000. And so I was in touch with my bank and made arrangements to finance the purchase for a figure around that level.

I notified Freeman & Co. that I would be in Philadelphia for the auction, and they informed me that I should bring a cashier's check for $25,000 and that my bids would then be accepted.

Joseph P. Driscoll, co-founder of Michigan General Corporation, and I were on a plane going to New York. I described the opportunity in detail and asked if he would be interested in buying the "Lost" Declaration copy as co-owner. He considered it and decided to do so.

Actually, we were going to New York to arrange for the public financing of our Michigan General Corporation, and so on the date of the auction we had an appointment with our lawyers in downtown Manhattan.

That seemed all right. I could see the lawyers in the morning and be in Philadelphia for the start of the auction at 1:30 that afternoon.

So at about 10:45 I announced that I had to be gone for a few hours, and went uptown to catch the train. I missed the 11 o'clock, and if I waited for the noon train I would not make it in time, I knew.

There was only one thing to do and that was to take a taxicab because I knew the driver could get there in time.

So I did, and although the taxi driver had never been to Philadelphia, he managed to get me to the place before the auction began.

I introduced myself to the auctioneers and told them I would sit on the far right of the third row and that my signal would be a movement of my right index finger near my right ear. If I moved that finger, it meant I was raising the bid by the precise amount of the prior increase, whatever that might be.

The bidding started at $100,000. It began jumping by $25,000 increments.

The most likely serious competitor seemed to be Hans P. Kraus, an important rare-book dealer from New York and chief of a large reprint publishing house in Liechtenstein. He wanted the document badly, and before leaving home that morning he had told his wife that he might have to pay half a million dollars for it. He had already paid $155,000 for a first printing of the Constitution, and since the Declaration was the oldest American document, and the rarest, he saw the value difference.

The $25,000 jumps continued until the bidding reached $225,000, and then it slowed. The other bidders began to drop out. There had been six. Soon there were three.

At $290,000 the third bidder dropped out and only Kraus and I were left in the contest.

For the 400 people it was becoming a tense show. They had been sitting quietly enough, but now you could hear the silence punctuated by sounds of awe and disbelief as the price continued to rise.

The bidding went up to $350,000 in increments of $10,000 and less. It nearly stopped at $350,000—Kraus gave serious consideration to dropping out then. He looked around to see who the other bidder was and could not find him.

The bidding went more slowly.

"$355,000," said Kraus.

I instantaneously wiggled my index finger near my right ear.

"I have $360,000," said Mr. Freeman, the auctioneer.

Kraus looked around the room again. He was puzzled. All the other bidders had been well-known dealers and he could not believe that an amateur could be making this big a play for the document.

"$365,000," said Kraus.

Again, immediately, my signal.

The bidding slowed down as Kraus continued to look around, annoyed. He raised in increments of $2,000, and then $1,000. But no matter what his raise was, I responded instantaneously and raised back the same amount.

At $375,000 Kraus became very agitated. He stopped and checked with the other dealers and determined that none of these was using a shill to bid against him. He may have thought the house was bidding the document up and insisted that he had a right to know the identity of the other bidder—if there was one.

Samuel T. Freeman flatly refused to tell him; they stood on their auctioneering reputation. Mr. Kraus could easily enough check the truthfulness of their statements. All he had to do, said Mr. Freeman, was stop bidding.

Again at $390,000 Kraus raised the issue. He continued to be agitated and finally gave an exasperated bid, when I had just touched my ear to raise it to $402,000.

"$403,000," he said.

I touched my ear again.

This time Kraus looked around again, and at the auctioneer, and then he shook his head.

Before he had left home that morning, when he told his

137

wife that he was thinking about paying a half-million for the Declaration, she had said, "Don't come home."

Now he could go home.

And I could go back to New York to finish my business with the lawyers and Joseph Driscoll. We had just bought the Declaration of Independence for $404,000. According to the Guinness Book of World Records, it is the highest price ever paid for a printed document.

27

The Corn-Driscoll Copy

The Corn-Driscoll copy of the Declaration of Independence has been widely shown over the years. It is also known as the "Lost" copy. It was displayed at a Junior Achievement Awards Banquet in Dallas, at the public library in Richardson, Texas, and during the Indianapolis Speedway Races festivities in May 1969. That year it was part of an exhibition to mark the dedication ceremony for the Douglas MacArthur Academy of Freedom at Howard Payne University, Brownwood, Texas.

In February 1970, we sent the declaration to the R. R. Donnelley & Sons Lakeside Press in Chicago to preserve the document in the best possible way and also to produce a facsimile on similar paper in a most faithful reproduction. We wanted to share with others the inspiration and heritage of the hallowed Declaration of Independence.

No expense was spared to create a realistic facsimile. A special paper was found that was almost identical to that used by John Dunlap in printing his original. The 1776 document has been printed on a hand letter press with a heavy impression that embossed the type slightly into the leaf. Lakeside Press matched that type of printing on a modern letter press.

To obtain the color of the aged paper and to reproduce the stains left by time, a deep-tone offset in three special colors was used. As a final touch, the facsimile was die-cut to match the rough edges of the slightly worn original document and to copy the slight deviation from a perfectly rectangular sheet of paper.

The result was a facsimile so realistic that a statement had to be printed on the back declaring that it was a copy, thus preventing confusion on the part of potential collectors.

This process took four months. Since the completion of the printing, several thousand facsimiles have been distributed to individuals, schools, museums, and other institutions across the nation to bring the message of American freedom to the citizens of the United States.

The original, in a newly designed frame, was displayed in 1970 at the Dallas Public Library "Heritage of Freedom" exhibit, the Dallas Museum of Fine Arts, and the Arkansas Museum of Fine Arts, Little Rock.

In the Summer of 1971 it was seen by visitors at a special exhibit built solely for that purpose for six months at the Chicago Museum of Science and Industry and later was part of the "Constitution Week" exhibit at the Republic National Bank of Dallas.

For their 1972 Continental Congress celebration in Washington, the Daughters of the American Revolution received permission to show the Declaration.

Approximately 1,700,000 persons who visited the California Museum of Science and Industry in Los Angeles saw the Corn-Driscoll Declaration during the period from June 1972 to February 1973.

Then the Declaration was taken to Expo '74 at Spokane, Washington, where 20,000 people lined up each day to visit it in the United States Department of Commerce exhibit. During that year the document also was on display at the DeSoto, Texas, Public Library and the Central Bank and Trust, Farmers Branch, Texas.

In the Spring of 1975 the Declaration was sent to the Library of Congress for a study by Frederick R. Goff, former Chief of the Rare Book Division, who was making a comparison of all known copies of the Dunlap broadside for a Bicentennial project of the Library of Congress. This book was published by the library in 1976.

One of the facsimiles of the Corn-Driscoll copy was featured by the Freedom Train on its nationwide tour from April 1975 to December 1976 and was seen in seventy-six cities in the forty-eight contiguous states.

In 1976, bicentennial year, exhibitions of the Corn-Driscoll copy were held at the First National Bank, Garland, Texas; the City Hall, Highland Park, Dallas, Texas; and the Chaparral Club meeting of the Friends of the Dallas Public Library. In June 1976, it became a most popular attraction at the American Booksellers Association Convention in Chicago.

Independence Day, bicentennial year, found the Corn-Driscoll copy on display at the South Street Seaport Museum in New York City as part of the Tall Ships weekend celebration. My daughter, Laura, was the official lecturer on the Declaration of Independence during the hectic Tall Ships occasion. She loved the response from the thousands who listened intently to the story.

For the months of August and September of 1976, it

was again part of a special display at the W. R. Grace Building in New York City.

It is no wonder that our copy is also known as the "traveling copy." It has been seen by more people since 1969 than made up the total population of the colonies in 1776; a tribute to the love and respect it has enjoyed for two hundred years.

28

The Meaning of the Declaration

In later years, when political opponents claimed sneeringly that Thomas Jefferson had not contributed anything very novel to the Declaration of Independence, he said that of course he had not. His function had been to draw together the body of American belief on the subject of basic liberties and mutual responsibilities.

He was well familiar with the one hundred and fifty year history of discord between the colonies and the mother country, and the resulting agreements and many drafts and redrafts of constitutions and bills of rights for various colonies over the years. Each of these contributed in its own way to the eventual ability of Congress to develop and agree on the Declaration of Independence.

In other words, the Declaration represents at least one hundred and fifty years of mutual experiment and experience in varying degrees of freedom under political control exercised by royal governors and the military.

Today we have no real vivid understanding of the common attitude in those days toward the ignorant, untrained, and indentured, the slaves, women, the uneducated, and the lowborn. We cannot visualize today just how little regard there was for the lives of these people, and how widely spread was the idea that they had no ability. Hence these groups had no responsibility in the management of affairs. For example, if they did not own property they could not vote.

There is no doubt, then, that the Declaration of Independence was written for the upper class, but with recognition even among the upper class that there was opportunity for extensive upward mobility. That is, the upper class was a meritocracy.

This is vastly different from the aristocracy approach, which confers importance only to those who are wellborn or are chosen by the wellborn. For example, when John Locke had served his masters well, those proprietors of the Carolinas colony, they offered him and his family in perpetuity a place in the Carolina aristocracy. That was the sort of thinking prevalent among the landed of England in the seventeenth century.

It was the potential of upward mobility of the citizens of the United States that was the entirely new factor in society. This attitude had grown during the one hundred and fifty years before the Revolution. The mobility was clearly pointed out by the success of the upper fifteen to twenty percent of the population. They were from the group from whence came the leaders as compared to an upper one percent, or less, as being their counterpart in Europe. They clearly recognized there was vast opportunity in the United States if they could unite and operate independently of England. The only way they could make the most of their opportunities was to make a clear break from England by means of revolution, a drastic step.

Therefore, even the most prosperous were willing finally to take a chance, and they did so against such high odds that we cannot even estimate them properly today.

The English army, for instance, was the best in the world. It had defeated everyone everywhere. The English navy was the best in the world, too. The intellectuals of England had freedom unequaled anywhere else in Europe. English industry led the Industrial Revolution.

And here were these children of England striking out on their own. The only thing that made it possible for them was many decades of success in forging growing cities and colonies out of the American wilderness. That history gave them the confidence, the ego, to rise up against England with its trained soldiers and its legitimacy in the eyes of the rest of the world.

The colonists had advantages not generally recognized in their mother country. They had overcome so many problems through the decades and had so many achievements that they had confidence. They had so much land developed, and so much remaining undeveloped, that they could see the future. They had so much trade to the point that the average colonial family had a better standard of living than the average family in England. In terms of rights, opportunity, and status, the colonist was incredibly better off than his English counterpart.

But they also had fears. The stakes were so enormous that the fainthearted were afraid. After all, they might lose everything if England proved to be bitter and revengeful if it were able to put down the rebelliousness of 1774–1776.

So one third of the colonists opposed the Revolution.

Also, most books that deal with the Declaration concentrate on Adams, Jefferson, and Franklin, which is natural enough since they were the framers. But few have pointed out that a majority of the delegates to Congress in 1775 opposed the Revolution. That is why it took a year to persuade the men of Congress that freedom from England was the only sensible course.

The best friend of the rebels was England itself, with its constant provocation and unwillingness to make the slightest concession. This played into the hands of Samuel Adams and the other hotheaded rebels.

To me it is important to know what Jefferson knew: that the Declaration of Independence did not develop out of a sudden inspiration or dream of a group of revolutionary geniuses. Instead, it was the result of more than a century of active movement in that direction, made possible by the lack of lines of authority between the crown and the colonies.

Spain, by the way, did not make that same mistake. Spain kept ironclad control of its colonies and did not provide its people the opportunity to grow and develop in the management of their own affairs.

Consequently, although Spain held control of some of its colonies until the twentieth century, not one of these had a background of freedom that made it possible for it to develop in the same manner as the United States. The revolutions of Latin America, the current troubles in the Philippines that have led to martial law, are a constant reminder of the failure or refusal of Spain to grant the same sort of freedoms to its colonists that the English did to the Americans.

The whole theory of personal freedom is based on the idea that if people are given freedom they will immediately make every possible decision in their own individual best interest. The composite result makes for a constructive and productive society.

And it was that way with the group of men at Philadelphia in 1776.

Most of them were either commercially successful or ambitious to be so. Each visualized that he would have more freedom to do what he wanted to do, and therefore succeed personally in a commercial way if not held back by British rules. Hence, each was in favor of freedom in the United States.

I have heard several discussions of the idea that commercial greed was the foundation of the Declaration of Independence, and eventually, the United States. I would place that motive above all others, but not because these people were selfish; rather because they observed that it worked best for all.

There were a few outright idealists, no doubt, but the principal purpose for founding a new nation was the continuation of the kind of personal freedom in support of economic opportunity that England gradually had permitted to develop in the colonies.

The progress of the black race from 1865 to the present day is a similar story. Beginning in 1954 with the Brown school desegregation decision, the blacks felt the breath of new personal freedom and, as a result, within a few years developed tremendous militancy.

During this period of great progress, one of the things that blacks were most militant about was their own question: "Why the devil did we wait so long?"

Blacks suddenly realized that if pushed, the society would give. But between the Civil War and the Brown decision, progress of blacks had been minuscule partially because they had not pushed.

It was the same way in every battle for personal freedom beginning in America. Between 1600 and 1776, as the people realized how productive it was to be free, they became more and more interested in the idea, even though those who gave them their freedom were constantly asking them, "Why don't you appreciate what we have done for you?"

"Why don't you remain loyal because none of this would have been possible without our being willing to give it to you," the English said.

But once having tasted freedom, the American people developed into a militant group who wanted to keep it. In the same way, the blacks between 1954 and today have evolved into a militant group, aggressively pushing what they should have been pushing long before.

And no doubt commercial success, or personal greed, or whatever it is called, contributed significantly to the success of Benjamin Franklin, John Adams, and Thomas Jefferson. The goal, however, was always personal freedom, with everyone competing for a share with no guarantee that anyone would win.

This was a vastly different concept from that in England, where the goal was for property and society to be specifically controlled by the aristocracy with no thought of equal opportunity for all those people who might vote on behalf of the winning group.

I have read that eighty percent of the adult men in America at the time of the Revolution were self-employed. Practically everyone was working for himself. Today eleven to twelve percent of the adult population is self-employed and more than triple that number are entrepreneurial in character. But vast numbers of people are continually moving into and out of that group. Anyone who wants to enter can do so.

The concept of personal freedom is not obsolete in the modern world of the technocrats and bureaucrats. Many government and political leaders would like to make us believe that it is necessary for all kinds of compromises

148

to be made in personal freedom, because otherwise there is no way to assure more egalitarianism.

This is another way of saying that many of our intellectuals believe it is better for everybody to have less—but more equally less—than to allow personal freedom full rein in terms of the rewards from upward mobility and success. They argue that if this happens then surely the range of economic differences between the high and the low become too great and unfair to the low.

The major proponent of this approach was Mao Tsetung in China. In that kind of society everyone becomes enmeshed in the beehive activity to suit a bureaucrat's desire, and personal freedom is barred altogether. The intellectual or bureaucrat who argues for that kind of control feels ultra-safe because he realizes that even in that type of society he will be one of the protected.

Yet, going back to our own history, we ought to recall that the American colonies were the most productive, most wealthy, and had the greatest amount of freedom of all British possessions. Cause for dissatisfaction existed less in North America than in any other of the colonies. Grievances were mild compared to discipline as it pertained to other colonies. Then the ensuing wealth of the colonies suddenly became obvious to England, which decided it was time the colonies should pay their share of expenditures, such as those for defense.

The colonies had never paid their share because, in essence, they were a developing nation. The leaders of the colonies realized that success had come from their own efforts. Therefore, they saw no reason for the fruits of success to be shared with the mother country.

No doubt commercial success was a major motivating objective. On July 6, 1776, the Dunlap copy of the Declaration was reproduced on the front page of the *Pennsylvania Post Gazette*. At the bottom of the page were ten advertisements from local businesses, which had absolutely nothing to do with the Declaration.

The point is that this was normal newspaper advertising of the day. Those who thought advertising began only with the recent period of American history may be surprised, but advertising has always been important in this country, although in the early days it was not as sophisticated as it is today.

So through that one hundred and fifty years before the Declaration of Independence, as each colony developed its own laws and institutions, many of those small holes in that giant screen were opening up. By the 1770s, the colonists realized that it was possible to operate a society whose authority and strength came from the consent of those who were governed. The Declaration of Independence catapulted the world up the steps toward the goal of maximum personal freedom.

In effect, the American Revolution occurred because long experience had proved that freedom could work. Consequently, Americans were prepared to fight to preserve what they had earned.

In many of today's societies a dictator often fights viciously to put down fires of freedom. He fears that if the people get too much of a taste of personal freedom they will demand more and more. England gave the colonies decades of experience in self-government and then found it was impossible to return them to a strictly dominated society.

Much of the same situation applies to others: the moment people in a society see it is possible for more and more freedom to be gained, they work harder to get more.

In the years following the Revolution, the owning of property as a prerequisite to voting was changed, debtors prisons were eliminated, slavery was ended, women won the vote, education became general, and hundreds of other steps were taken to enlarge the amount of personal and economic freedom. Today we enjoy more freedom than any other society, and yet we are still a long way from achieving perfection.

The Declaration of Independence presented an original concept. It was an exciting result of all that had gone before, an outburst of the surge for freedom that soon thereafter began to move around Europe.

The Constitution was the document that translated that concept into the real world. Out of all the achievements of the Declaration of Independence and the Constitution, the one that was most significant in providing for a free society's existence was the fragmentation of police power.

In the study of those one hundred and fifty years before the Declaration, there is specific significance in the development of the fragmentation of police power as it affected the general citizenry. For example, today our country has several types of police authority. It has the army and the navy, the National Guard, the FBI and the Treasury agents, police under the authority of the organized community, village, township, city, county, and the federal and state marshals who carry out orders of the courts. This fragmentation prevents any one political force from gaining control over another.

The United States is the only country in the world today in which the police power is thus fragmented. What facilitated the takeovers of authority by Indira Gandhi in India and Ferdinand Marcos in the Philippines is the fact that the police powers of those nations were at their disposal as the chief executives. For decades Europeans have known that the single most important office in their governments was that which had charge of the police. By replacing members of the police hierarchy with those who support the politician, no leader ever need give up con-

151

trol. He merely announces that he will ignore any election plans or demands, and the general population is helpless.

The term "police power" means force exercised by government. It includes the regular army and, on top of that, the various police agencies. But coercion, except on a localized basis, is impossible to achieve when police power is fragmented. One politician can control one city or a state, but he cannot gain control over several cities and states. Because the federal bureaucracy has no local police powers, the United States has a government with this key built-in restraint.

In the United States we also have fragmented leadership, unlike the situation that exists in the other Western democracies. In countries such as England, the power of the ruling party is tied to the success of the office of prime minister. In the United States each congressman, senator, governor, etc., has the protection of a fixed term of office with the electorate being the judge of the ability and success of each. Because thousands of private citizens throughout our nation desire to serve in key governmental positions, and thus to lead, there exists a competition for leadership in the United States. This serves the cause of freedom much better than the discipline of a two-party system with all members forced to follow the official leader.

The meaning of the Declaration, though, can easily enough be shown in two incidents that occurred in the days of the revolutionaries and earlier.

First was an incident, or a combination of them, that began in 1732, some forty years before the Revolutionary War. King George II granted a charter to James Oglethorpe to provide in Georgia a haven for debtors and victims of religious persecution. Oglethorpe and his fellow trustees decided that their humanitarian goals could best be achieved by a system of thorough regimentation.

The land was divided, and each citizen of the new colony was granted a 500-acre holding.

These parcels could not be divided, sold, rented, traded, mortgaged, or even passed down in the family. Regulations began to pile up about the land use, and the problems of the people piled right on top of them.

After two years, in an effort to gain trust and support in the colonies, the trustees declared:

"This board will always do what is right. The people should have confidence in us."

(That sounds like the voice of government today.)

One of the more fantastic programs of the economic planners of Georgia involved silk cultivation. Each settler was required to plant fifty trees and produce a certain quantity of silk. Unless he produced that given quantity, he could neither vote nor hold public office.

But the main flaw was that the silkworms brought to Georgia could not survive in that climate, and they died just as fast as they were imported.

Even so, the scheme went on for twenty years before the bureaucrats admitted failure. Then, after those twenty years of mismanagement, the charter was returned to the crown. By this time most of the settlers had left. They had voted with their feet. And then economic planning ended in Georgia. Twenty years later it was a prosperous colony and the population had increased eightfold.

Now let us turn northward for a moment. The Declaration of Independence has been signed; it is September 15, 1776. The British have just landed their redcoats and they have come to the intersection of Thirty-second Street and East River Drive in Manhattan Island (which then, of course, was a country lane). The landing has been preceded by a bombardment that has destroyed the fortifications of General George Washington and the revolutionary army. Washington is already in deep trouble. He

153

has just escaped from Long Island, where he suffered a serious defeat when one of his generals left a major road unguarded.

The cause of the Revolution looks hopeless. Barely over two months ago Washington caused the Declaration of Independence to be read to these troops. Now they are wondering if it is worth it.

The British general Lord Howe, has also read the Declaration, the copy of the Dunlap broadside he captured during the summer. But he now feels that he has Washington in his power, that the Americans will have to surrender in a matter of days or be roundly defeated.

Washington retreats this day to Harlem Heights on the West Side of Manhattan Island (now the site of Columbia University). Howe pursues.

And now Howe's advance guard comes to the farmhouse of Judith Sargent Murray and her two daughters, who know the Declaration of Independence just as well as anyone in the colonies. Without a tremor these ladies entertain the British officers and insist that they stay for tea.

And while they pour the tea and chatter at the redcoated gentlemen, Washington and his forces escape the trap. Historians disagree on some of the details of this story, but there is no doubt about the impact of this and thousands of similar incidents which dot the history pages of our war for independence.

I like the story. It is a great illustration of what the Declaration of Independence meant in its own day.

29

Impact of the Declaration

One of the little-recognized reasons the Declaration of Independence became such an outstanding success was that it was a non-operating document.

All the parties involved knew the Declaration to be an expression of intent, opinion, and idealism, and that it did not tackle the most important job of directing the way the various colonies were to live.

Judges will never be called upon to interpret its clauses. Contracts do not have to be judged by its authority. This condition was a major asset in many respects. For example, it enabled all the colonies to allow slavery to continue while declaring an absolute opposite attitude toward the institution in its broad purpose clauses. Since the Declaration did not pursue the problem of property rights or voting restrictions, it was able to gain support from everyone involved because it has such effective language, expressing deep-seated human desires in an incredibly responsive manner.

This was a rallying cry, a document that all those who believed in the Revolution could support even though later there might be sharp and distinctive differences in the implementation of the document's principles.

The Declaration's inconsistency with the principle of slavery was recognized, but after Jefferson's clause attacking slave trade was removed by mutual consent, no confrontation on the issue occurred. The price that had to be paid eighty-odd years later as a result of this weakness proved to be a bloody one and was, no doubt, the Declaration's principal liability. No agreement could have been reached, however, between the thirteen colonies had there been a showdown in 1776.

Slavery proved to be a monument to the ability of man to rationalize his absurdities.

Those who signed for the colonies that practiced slavery did so by rationalizing to themselves that slaves were not men, and therefore the assertion in the Declaration that all men are equal did not apply to slaves. This was considered so obvious to everyone that it was not necessary to rationalize the inconsistencies. The signers chose to ignore the situation that existed in some colonies: there were slaves who had been given all their rights and made free men. What was the difference between these people and the other blacks who lived in bondage?

The signers of the Declaration rationalized this as an aberration of society and one that need not even be explained away.

Those colonists who were against slavery were just as foolish in their attitude; they believed that if ignored, the problem would disappear or subside until it could be solved on some unknown basis. In the meantime, they would make this compact with the citizens of the slave-owning states because the struggle against a common enemy had the highest priority at the moment. On both sides there was this obvious compromise. In effect, the date on which the problem would be resolved was postponed, or in the parliamentary sense, "laid on the table," without reference and without formal action.

The colonies were so badly split on the issue of slavery that had they tried to resolve it, the Declaration might have foundered. They knew, too, that if they attempted to fight independently against England the odds were astronomically high that the Revolution would fail. Whatever chance they had, they agreed, existed only for a United Thirteen Colonies.

It was, as Ben Franklin was supposed to have said at the end of the exhausting proceedings, a very simple matter.

"We must all hang together," he said. "For if we do not, we most certainly shall all hang separately."

Later, when the Articles of Confederation were written, many significant issues emerged to show how far apart the thirteen colonies really were. Again, compromises were made, but because the Articles comprised an operating document, they failed. They had produced a weak government. It became apparent that a stronger document of agreement would have to be written if there was going to be a successful United States of America.

My interest in the Declaration of Independence has always been from the point of view that ideas control man and that the concept of personal freedom was so clearly enunciated in the Declaration of Independence that all subsequent efforts to cut back on personal freedom and individualism eventually failed.

The Constitution of the United States originally called for the election of senators by state legislatures. This, too, was a reflection of the old system of duality of power: a

157

privileged class (senators) and a popular class (representatives). It denied elective power to the citizens and gave it to legislators, who were supposedly the elite, and who were actually one step removed from the body politic. Eventually this restriction was abolished by constitutional amendment. The Civil War solved the worst problem.

For nearly one hundred and fifty years women did not have the right to vote. This roadblock in their path to freedom was also swept away by constitutional amendment.

Child labor was abolished. The right to join unions was institutionalized. Voting rights were broadened.

In 1954 the nation and the courts began to put teeth into antidiscrimination action with the end result that the institution of segregation is being overcome. Then the right to vote was extended to eighteen-year-olds.

Throughout the two hundred year period since the signing of the Declaration of Independence, continual attacks have been made on the press by various government authorities. Despite some temporary successes, ultimately all these have failed and freedom of the press has increased rather than declined.

We have seen the effectiveness of the idea of personal freedom. I suggest as a startling conclusion that the amount of personal and human freedom today in America is more than tenfold greater than it was in the first ten years of the life of the United States of America. The Declaration of Independence established the spirit that allowed personal freedom to grow steadily throughout the past two hundred years. It is not merely a matter of holding on to the freedoms that were ordained by the Declaration of Independence and the Constitution. It is a matter of nurturing freedom to attain greater growth because much work remains to make personal freedom more perfectly realized. The essential elements for making possible continued growth of personal freedom are equal opportunity, equal economic opportunity, and the continued improvement in the quality of justice and the rights of individuals. Perhaps man will never find perfection in his quest for freedom. It is not important that he does. It is only important that, as the years go by, greater effort is made to provide more freedom each day than we had yesterday, and more tomorrow than we enjoy today. For two hundred years each succeeding generation has had its own impact on the growth of this condition. Our history includes many periods of severe setbacks and other periods of accelerated improvement. Just a few of the negative periods worth mentioning include the Ku Klux Klan era, the period of separate but equal educational facilities for blacks, "the Great Depression," the World War II placement of Japanese-American citizens in concentration camps, and the era of fear during which Senator Joseph McCarthy dominated Washington.

Our Founding Fathers were well aware that, historically, government has always been a word for tyranny. In simple language, government has the power to tell us what we can and cannot do, backed up by enough force to see that we follow directions.

Because of our positive, favorable view of government, we have, in too many cases, been willing to turn over matters of consequence to government control. Many view government as an all-knowing father, who with fairness and justice will resolve our problems. This concept has been more successful in the United States than in most other societies.

The complexity of life requires society to have far more government today than it had two hundred years or even fifty years ago. Only by uniting through government agencies can society protect itself against the abuse of natural resources, economic concentration, environmental, and international danger. This has nothing to do with whether the government is liberal or conservative. It has to do with turning over responsibility for society's decisions to third parties instead of being responsible for these decisions ourselves. As society shifts the decision-making responsibility, personal freedom tends to deteriorate. The bureaucrat, who is speaking for the government and who is anxious to receive authority, believes, with good intentions, that his decisions are going to be better than anyone else's.

But if anything is proven in history, it is that this is not the case. The bureaucrat is subject to the same whims of human nature that everyone else is: avarice, greed, power, poor decision making, ego, and the willingness to use force to have things his way.

Yes, I believe the enemy has always been government, whether a monarchy, dictatorship, or a democracy. There is always the temptation for leaders to usurp power or to persuade and bribe the voters into turning over responsibility to them in an effort to improve the decision-making results. In all events, government represents force and force is the opposite of personal freedom.

The problem, of course, is to find that middle ground which, for two hundred years, the United States has been fortunate in finding more often than any other society.

Also, history tells us that the battle is never won. It is always underway. The reasons are found within us. Human nature has a dark side. People have a deep-seated desire to have things their own way. If given authority and responsibility, many political leaders who profess a love for democracy and personal freedom would quickly subordinate that love to a preference for having things their way.

The United States' social and economic system is the greatest in the world in terms of opportunity open to more people at all social and economic levels than any other society. One can often read comments to the contrary. They are not true. It is true that our system is not perfect—nowhere nearly perfect—but it is still far more perfect than any other system and our society continues to improve because we have never ceased our search for more equality in freedom, economic opportunity, and justice.

Cromwell rode to power in England with the cry of overthrowing the tyrant Charles I. Within a few short years, Cromwell himself had become a tyrant more powerful than any England had ever experienced. On both large and small scales, within political and human institutions, this same story has been repeated millions of times.

The Declaration of Independence has been a unique exception—a document that continues to live. During those critical years when the Constitution was being written and subsequently approved by Constitutional assemblies elected expressly for that purpose throughout the thirteen colonies, political leaders often turned to the inspiration of the Declaration of Independence to encourage approval of the Constitution.

So perhaps it was better that the Declaration of Independence never was an operating document, that it has never been quoted for its authority to support legislation, and never used by the courts in interpreting that which was Constitutional and that which was not. Even today in reading the Preamble, one may feel the challenge inspired by those magic words:

"When in the course of human events, it becomes necessary for one people to dissolve the political bands, which have connected them with another, and to assume, among the powers of the earth, the separate and equal station, to which the laws of nature and of nature's God entitle them, a decent respect to the opinions of mankind requires that they should declare the causes which impel them to the separation.

"We hold these truths to be self-evident, That all men are created equal, that they are endowed by their Creator with certain unalienable rights; that among these are life, liberty, & the pursuit of happiness; that to secure these rights governments are instituted among men, deriving their just powers from the consent of the governed; that whenever any form of government becomes destructive of these ends, it is the right of the people to alter or abolish it, and to institute new government, laying its foundation on such principles and organizing its powers in such form, as to them shall seem most likely to effect their safety and happiness. . . ."

It was de Tocqueville, the famous French writer, fifty years later who said, "If democracy and personal freedom are ever to operate throughout the world it will have to be through governments founded on constitutions similar to that of the United States. Unless government's powers are restricted, eventually government falls to force."

Constitutions written throughout the rest of the world in the two hundred years since 1776 have had very poor results, often because the leaders of those nations involved failed to live up to their obligations under their constitution. Other failures have occurred because of the citizens' lack of experience with the concept of a constitution and similar human institutions. Without the thousands of experiments in personal freedom, controversies, and documents which dotted the history of all thirteen colonies prior to 1776, it is unlikely that the United States Constitution and the Declaration of Independence would have lived as successfully as they have for the past two hundred years.

No society that has ever attempted to form a constitutional-based government should give up because it failed the first time or the second or the third. Our experience clearly proves they should try again and again, because in the trying, success will eventually come.

As personal and economic freedom have grown since the Declaration of Independence, so have their benefits. The more the power of increased personal freedom has been turned loose, the more productive it has become. It has helped to produce an economy of incredible size and a people of such widespread affluence and high cultural standards that even the living standards of those in the poverty class exceed those of the vast majority of the rest of the world. Because of the upper mobility potential in our society, there has been no monopoly of opportunity by any group remotely resembling a self-perpetuating class. Thus, in our efforts to make maximum use of personal freedom and equal opportunity, we have faced no class struggle. In many ways our government has been an essential element in helping to create an open society in terms of personal freedom and equal opportunity, and much of this has been accomplished without encroaching whatsoever on the creed of the Declaration of Independence for increased personal freedom.

163

30

Epilogue

It has long been assumed that the search for religious freedom brought vast numbers of Englishmen across the Atlantic to these undeveloped shores. In truth, however, it was the hope for economic gain which gave the original impetus to the development of wilderness lands of what was to become the United States.

England's claim to a major portion of the North American continent was well established from the time of John Cabot's explorations in 1497. However, for over a century very little was done about implementing this claim. It was only in 1606 with the chartering of the Virginia Company as a private enterprise that the English began to develop their country's claim successfully. For some time they had been immigrating to Ireland but greater opportunities were soon to be perceived in North America. The hope was to sell land and thus make money by colonizing the New

World and, at the same time, eliminate what was then comprehended to be a problem of overcrowding in Great Britain itself, although the population by 1600 was only about 4,000,000 persons.

Prior to 1640 virtually all of the colonization and exploration came as the result of the funding of eleven privately owned and managed joint stock companies. Thousands of Englishmen who were the stockholders of these publicly owned companies had a significant stake in the colonies as a result of their investments. In the meantime, those colonists whose motives to immigrate were more religious than economic were taking advantage of the stock companies' efforts.

The stock companies had several unique characteristics unlike their modern counterparts. In those days holders of stock were not only liable for the investment but also for all liabilities. The concept of limited liability in privately owned corporations had not yet developed. The impact of this rule meant that the companies were planned to have a short life as efforts were pushed to pay back stockholders. While the Crown was willing to help the colonies by granting Royal Charters with colorful rights and goals, the United States as we know it today was founded basically upon the drive to make a dollar.

More than 200,000 Englishmen immigrated in the first half of the seventeenth century. Contrast those figures to those of Spain where, in the entire 300 years of Spanish management ownership and development of Spanish America, only 300,000 Spanish citizens immigrated to the New World.

The English Crown at the start psychologically lost its outright claim to the American colonies because it was not royal money which founded the colonies. Instead it was through funds raised by entrepreneurs and investors.

True, charters from the Crown had to be obtained, but that was merely paper. Thereafter the English kings were always sensitive to the charge that they should not object to approving frequently requested changes in those charters since it was not their money originally that caused the colonies to be founded.

As reflected in the next chapter which highlights the 170 years of colonization, from 1606 to 1776, they were far from tranquil times. It was a long period of dispute, argument, rebellion, feuding, and constant pressure for more rights for the colonists. Realistically, the only time the Redcoats were welcome in the colonies was when France represented a danger. The desire for freedom was growing and finally reached a point in 1776 when outright rebellion could no longer be postponed.

The most important characteristic of the colonies during this lengthy and evolving period was the development by local government at local levels and the growing acceptance of legal justice as determined in local courts. This early fragmentation of political power into several thousand decentralized political units was the foundation for the present structure of our city, county, state, and federal government. Justification of the theory was based on the idea that those citizens who paid the taxes should make the decisions and that the closer the level of decision making was to those who paid the taxes the more equitable the government was likely to be. Hence school boards began passing local taxes to support local schools; city councils levied local taxes to support city government; states (colonies) taxed to support state government; and later, the federal government had another set of taxes for its purposes. Because the decisions over spending the money were made at the local level, talented people were attracted to participate in each local government entity.

In virtually all other nations of the world, the leading law firms, architects, engineers, and financial specialists of all kinds operate out of the national capital where the money-spending decisions are made. In the United States this is not true. In all the major cities throughout the United States many successful political and economic leaders and other specialists can be found. This decentralization of talent has been of immense philosophical value to a democratic government and to the cause of personal freedom because the defenders of that freedom are talented people everywhere, not just in the national capital. It is important to note that this decentralization of talent tracks the decentralization of tax collecting.

Throughout the history of the United States continuing charges have been made that freedom is being reduced as federal government becomes more centralized. Oftentimes, however, those who make the charge relate change to a lessening of personal freedom. Established society tends to resist change; hence any change proposed is often judged as a reduction of freedom when in fact it may only be a change in society's accepted customs. For example, at the time laws against child labor were first proposed it was customary and part of naturally accepted rules of society that 95 percent of the children worked. Any prohibition of child labor at first sounded un-American. It soon became obvious that the proposed laws were sound and the country was affluent enough to withdraw child labor from that segment of the working population without unreasonable cost to society. Today we look back upon that period as some kind of ghastly phase of human development. But in fact it was the custom because previous societies had always needed for children to work for survival. The United States was fortunate enough to be able to eventually do away with child labor and today all but the most extreme advocate of pure personal freedom would say that the right decision was made.

Much the same can be said today about the very sincere and generous desire of most Americans to provide for the disadvantaged, the helpless, and the weak. In all surveys made on the subject at least 80 percent of all Americans are in favor of government efforts for the benefit of those who are helpless and in real need of assistance. Some would say that to pass heavy taxes to provide this support is a blow against personal freedom. In fact, it is a change in human custom rather than a blow to personal freedom.

This is not to say that all such efforts by government fall within that category. For example, efforts to "tell people" what to do or to protect them from themselves are certainly on the border line and would fall within the danger point because this is a retreat back to the acceptance of autocratic authority. When an agency, a bureaucrat, or Congress itself decides that such and such personal behavior is "best for everyone" and enacts a decree to that effect, that clearly represents an invasion of personal freedom. There is a dark side in human nature to want to impose an opinion on others. It has always been so and always will be. This surfaces when people in authority are given the right to tell people "what is best for them." My own judgment is that the American people are very quick to appreciate this danger and that government tendencies in this direction will fail much the same as people who refuse to pay attention automatically to those in their private lives, for example, parents who wish to tell their children "what is best for them."

There is absolutely no doubt that in the 170 years prior to 1776 there was a fantastic and incredible growth of personal freedom and economic opportunity which led directly to the Revolution. In the past 200 years this freedom has been marked by continued growth beyond anyone's fondest imagination. Of course, my estimate that there has been a ten-times increase in personal freedom since 1776 is subject to considerable debate, but whether it is five times, ten times, or fifteen times is not important. That the trend is in that direction and is sound makes us a model for all societies to observe. And that is what the Declaration of Independence is all about. It was the catalyst, the giant step forward that crystallized the American Dream, not just for Americans, but for all who cared to learn.

Chronological Listing of the Highlights of the 170 Years' March for Independence Culminating in the Declaration of Independence in 1776

1606—The Virginia Company was chartered for profit in London for the purpose of organizing a settlement in Virginia in order to make money. His Majesty's government granted the charter provided all the funds were raised privately. The United States was born by means of selling stock in England. This set the stage for the philosophical future of the United States of America. (Bailyn, pp. 37–38)

1607, May 14—"First permanent English settlement in America begun at Jamestown, Virginia." (Kull, p. 18)

1608—John Smith had two Indians tell him how to raise Indian corn. Faced with starvation, colonists accepted this new grain although opposition to it existed everywhere. (Carruth, pp. 5–7)

1608—First "American" book (written by John Smith) was entitled *A True Relation of Such Occurrences and Accidents of Noate as Hath Hapned in Virginia Since the*

First Planting of That Colony. Printed in London. (Carruth, p. 4) Just as the Spaniards who explored and conquered the southern part of the hemisphere broadcast the news and description of that place to their fellow Europeans, so too did some of the early English arrivals.

1609 (Spring)—"John Smith gets forty acres into cultivation. Raising of corn learned from Indians." (Kull, p. 19) Perhaps a first step in independence was in learning how to live in the new land; eventually achieving economic strength and the ability to survive without dependence on English goods, supplies, or previous living habits. Through adaptation the settlers achieved a new identity and eventually became "Americans"—people of a new hemisphere and not transplanted Englishmen.

1609, May 23—"London Company obtains new royal charter, incorporating the original London patentees as a joint stock company and bestowing upon them land and rights of government hitherto reserved to the king. Henceforth commonly known as Virginia Company, Sir Thomas Smith appointed treasurer." (Kull, p. 20)

1614—"Sir Thomas Dale allots three-acre holdings to settlers in Virginia, beginning of system of private holdings." (Kull, p. 22)

1618 (Summer)—Sir Edwin Sandys of the Virginia Company formulates his plan for the government of the colony. Among the principles included in the plan was the idea that no government should be instituted without the consent of the colonists. (Corn, pp. 21–22)

1618, November 18—"Charter of privileges, orders, and laws granted Virginia settlers by Virginia Company in London, giving them voice in making of laws." (Kull, p. 22)

1619, July 30—Virginia House of Burgesses meets in Jamestown for the first time, enacts the "Charter of Grants and Liberties" (Sir Edwin Sandys' plan). This was the first representative law-making body in English America, its purpose being to enact "wholesome laws and ordinances pertaining to the safety and welfare of the colony." (Andrews, p. 32; Chitwood, pp. 79–80; Wright, p. 10)

1620—"First public library in British colonies established at projected college in Heunco, Virginia." Library flourished through bequests of books from English estates. (Carruth, p. 8)

1620, November 11—Mayflower Compact signed in Provincetown Harbor, first written constitution in colonies, Plymouth, Massachusetts. The Mayflower's destination had been south of the Hudson River. The actual area where the Puritans disembarked was beyond the bounds of the sponsoring company in London. Thus, the Mayflower Compact was drawn up to serve as a provisional instrument of government until more permanent forms could be adopted. Has been called "the foundation of American democracy" although in itself the Compact was not originally very democratic. (In modern terms, of course, lack of religious freedom, for example.) (*NYT Almanac,* p. 268)

1620, November 21—The significance of the Mayflower Compact lies in the fact that it set up "a civil body politic" to frame "just and equal laws" as a preliminary plan of government in the Colony. (Morris, p. 31)

1621—"Congregational system of church government introduced at Plymouth by Pilgrims." (Kull, p. 24) Since congregationalism is defined as having the emphasis on the "right and responsibility of each properly organized congregation to make its own decisions about its own affairs, without having to submit them to the judgment of any higher human authority" (Britannica, Vol. 6, 1973, p. 322), the founding fathers in adopting this form set the precedent for independent management of their lives which contributed to the general development toward political independence.

1621, July 24—"Ordinance and Constitution for Virginia government granted by Virginia Company." (Kull, p. 24) In 1624 the charter for Virginia Company was revoked "after long conflict with liberal elements in Company" (Kull, p. 26), and later was restored March 26, 1628 (e.g., House of Burgesses).

1629, March 14—The Massachusetts Bay Company "received a royal charter which specified no location for its annual meeting. This oversight made it possible to transfer the government to New England and transform the company into a self-governing commonwealth." (Morris, p. 33)

1629, August 26—"Cambridge Agreement signed by twelve members of Massachusetts Bay Company, pledging themselves to migrate to New England if the charter may be taken with them." (Kull, p. 27)

1630, March 29—"Puritans with John Winthrop, governor of Massachusetts Bay Company, sail for New England . . . carrying the company's charter with them." (Kull, p. 28)

1630, August 23—"Winthrop's court of assistants orders wage ceiling of two shillings a day in building trades. First legislation in America to affect free labor." (Kull, p. 28)

1630, October 19—"A general court, first in New England, held in Boston; 108 settlers appear before it demanding admission as freemen of Massachusetts Bay Company." (Kull, p. 28)

1632—Watertown, Massachusetts, protests the payment of taxes levied by the board of assistants to fortify Newtown, claiming that the power to make laws and levy taxes belongs to the people. (Chitwood, p. 135). Cecilius

Calvert, second Baron Baltimore, granted the colony of Maryland (which had originally been granted to his father, the first Baron Baltimore, George Calvert). The grant was made by Charles I. Calvert who began to develop his province as an income source (not in the least unusual) and as a "religious haven for persecuted fellow Catholics." (*NYT Almanac*, p. 267)

1632, May 9—"Massachusetts Bay General Court orders that a board composed of two delegates from each town shall guide governor and assistants in levying taxes. Result of Watertown protest." (Kull, p. 29)

1633—"Adam Roelantsen arrives in New Amsterdam to start a school, beginning of education in settlement." (Kull, p. 29)

1634, May 14—"Massachusetts Bay Colony establishes representative system of government after deputies from its towns demand to see charter of Company." (Kull, p. 30)

1635—Boston Latin School, one of the first grammar schools in America, opened. (*NYT Almanac*, p. 53)

1635—"Symms Free School, established by legacy of Benjamin Symms in Elizabeth City County, is Virginia's first school." (Kull, p. 30)

1635, February 26—"Maryland assembly of all freemen of colony convenes without authority of Lord Baltimore and drafts code which he disallows." (Kull, p. 30)

1635, April—"Governor John Harvey of Virginia deposed by council and sent to England because of his support of Lord Baltimore in controversy with Claiborne and his disregard of privileges of Virginia Assembly." (Kull, p. 30)

1635, October 9—"Roger Williams preaching separation of Church and State, banished from Massachusetts Bay by General Court." (Kull, p. 30)

1636—Banished in 1635 from the Massachusetts Bay

Colony, Roger Williams founds Providence, Rhode Island, the first English colony to grant religious freedom. (*NYT Almanac,* p. 53)

1636—"First pensions in America awarded to wounded soldiers by Plymouth Pilgrims." (Carruth, p. 12)

1636—The Plymouth Colony General Court "comprised two deputies from each town chosen by the freemen together with the Governor and assistants sitting as a single house." Early form of representative government in the New World. (Morris, p. 32)

1636, March 3—"Township Act, passed by General Court of Massachusetts Bay grants powers of government to freemen of the towns." (Kull, p. 30)

1636, March 3—"Majority vote of both assistants and deputies required for all acts by Massachusetts Bay General Court." (Kull, p. 30)

1636, October 28—"Harvard College founded by vote of General Court of Massachusetts Bay which appropriates 400 pounds for it." (Kull, p. 31)

1636, November 15—"Plymouth colony adopts code of laws, first in New England." (Kull, p. 31)

1637, August 20—The Providence Compact. "We whose names are hereunder, desirous to inhabit in the town of Providence, do promise to subject ourselves in active or passive obedience to all such orders or agreements that shall be made for public good of the body in an orderly way by the major consent of the present inhabitants, masters of families, incorporated together into a town fellowship, and others who may shall admit unto them *only in civil things.*" It was the first social contract for government into which the principle of complete religious liberty was written. (Carroll, p. 70)

1638—"Representative government adopted by Plymouth Colony." (Kull, p. 31)

1638—First document printed by Stephen Day on the first printing press in English colonies was the famous broadsheet *Oath of a Freeman.* It reads in part: "I doe solemnly bind myself in the sight of God, that when I shal be called to give my voyce touching any such matter of this State, in which Freemen are to deal, I will give my vote and suffrage as I shall judge in mine own conscience and tend to the publicke weal of the body, without respect of persons, or favour of any man." (Carruth, p. 14)

1638, April 15—"New Haven founded by Theophilus Eaton and John Davenport, without charter or land grant." (Kull, p. 32)

1639—"Stephen Day sets up first printing press in English colonies, at Cambridge, Massachusetts." (Kull, p. 32)

1639—"First post office established by Massachusetts Bay General Court in house of Richard Fairbank in Boston." (Kull, p. 32)

1639—"Each town in Massachusetts Bay ordered by General Court to lay out roads connecting it with the next." (Kull, p. 32)

1639—"Margaret Brent appeared before Maryland Assembly and requested right to vote, an unprecedented, in fact, unheard of gesture for a woman of this time." (Carruth, p. 15) Also see year 1640 for more on this woman.

1639, January 14—"Fundamental orders of Connecticut adopted by freemen of Windsor, Wethersfield and Hartford, first written constitution in history detailing functions of government." (Kull, p. 32) In Connecticut the "Fundamental Orders" are adopted which "gave citizens the right to elect public officials and omitted the usual religious test for citizenship." (*NYT Almanac,* p. 251)

1639, February 12—In Maryland the Third Assembly meets. In preparation the governor had called the first free elections in the colony's history. This third assembly established the House of Assembly whose members would represent the freemen of Maryland "as do the Burgesses in the House of Commons" in England. (Chalmers, p. 9; Dozer, pp. 57–58)

1640—"Bay Psalm Book published by Stephen Day at Cambridge, first book published in the English settlements of America." (Kull, p. 33)

1640—"Mistress Margaret Brent, colonial attorney for Cecilius Calvert, Lord Proprietor of Maryland, became first lady barrister in America." (Carruth, p. 17) Also see year 1647.

1640—"Boston Common reserved for use of municipality in maintaining some natural retreat for city dwellers." (Carruth, p. 16)

1641—Massachusetts adopts the "Bodies of Liberties," a code of laws established "in order that the people might know what were their rights and duties, and that the judges might be bound to definite principles in rendering their decisions." (Becker, p. 99; Chitwood, third edition, 1961, p. 114)

1641, June 2—"General Court of Massachusetts Bay grants the towns power to regulate prices of commodities and wages." (Kull, p. 33)

1641, October—"Sam Windslow of Massachusetts granted first patent in colonics for a process of manufacturing salt, the term of this patent to extend ten years." (Carruth, p. 17)

1641, December 10—"Body of Liberties, a code of laws, adopted by General Court of Massachusetts Bay colony." (Kull, p. 33)

1642—"Care of the poor by each town enacted by Plymouth colony." (Kull, p. 33)

1642, June 14—"Massachusetts law of 1642 empowers

177

town authorities to punish parents and guardians who fail to train their children in reading and principles of religion." (Kull, p. 33)

1643—"Lord Baltimore, to attract settlers, sends notice to New England that all creeds will be protected in Maryland." (Kull, p. 34)

1643—"Cosmopolitan nature of New York City's population had early beginning. Although administered by Dutch until 1674, there were over twenty different nationalities and sects on Manhattan Island in 1643, speaking eighteen different languages." (Carruth, p. 16) Religious toleration and commercial activity further encouraged this situation.

1643, March 2—"Virginia adopts act denying right of governor and council to impose taxes without consent of assembly." (Kull, p. 34)

1643, May 19—"New England Confederation formed by colonies of Massachusetts Bay, Plymouth, Connecticut, and New Haven, a league for offense and defense." (Kull, p. 34)

1643, October 27—"New Haven colony drafts constitution for representative government." (Kull, p. 34)

1644—"Probably first great democratic note struck in colonies is Roger Williams' *The Bloudy Tenent of Persecution for Cause of Conscience,* which asserted that basis of power lies in people and 'that such Governments as are by them erected and established have no more power, nor for no longer time, than the civill power or people consenting and agreeing shall betrust them with.' Being regarded as a dangerous book, was burned by public hangman in London. Fortunately, Williams did not sign his name to it." (Carruth, p. 18)

1644, March 7—"Bicameral system of legislature adopted by Massachusetts Bay." (Kull, p. 34)

1644, November 13—"Massachusetts Bay General Court directs county courts to have Indians in their shires instructed in knowledge and worship of God." (Kull, p. 34)

1647—Rhode Island outlaws trials for witchcraft and imprisonment for debt. (Wright, p. 11)

1647, January—"Margaret Brent initiated women suffrage movement after she had demanded right to vote in Maryland Assembly. Though outspoken and vociferous, she was refused." (Carruth, p. 19)

1647, November 11—"Massachusetts Law of 1647 requires every town of fifty householders to employ a teacher of reading and writing, and every town of one hundred families to establish a grammar school." (Kull, p. 35)

1648—"Earliest recorded orphan's court in America held in Virginia. It delegated administration of orphans' estates to guardians and heard complaints against such guardians." (Carruth, p. 19)

1648—"Laws and Liberties of Massachusetts published. A revision of Body of Liberties of 1641." (Kull, p. 35)

1648, October 18—"Massachusetts Bay Colony authorized first labor organization in U.S. 'The shoomakers of Boston' were permitted to meet whenever they wanted to choose officers and clerks." (Carruth, p. 18)

1649, April—Maryland Assembly convenes and passes the famous "Act of Religious Freedom" which referred to the dangers of enforcing conscience and asserted that no Christian should be denied free exercise of his religion. (Chalmers, p. 78; Fisher, p. 70; Dozer, p. 87)

1650—Maryland constitution permanently established; no taxes to be levied on freemen without their consent or that of their representatives in assembly; martial law not to be executed except in time of war; freemen win right to propose and approve legislation.

1650, April 6—"Maryland granted by Lord Baltimore

a two-house assembly, lower house of delegates and upper house of councillors." (Kull, p. 36)

1650, May—"Laws of Connecticut codified, modeled upon Body of Liberties of Massachusetts Bay." (Kull, p. 36)

1652—"Boston's first book store opened." (Kull, p. 37)

1652, April—"Peter Stuyvesant forced to grant New Amsterdam autonomous city government." (Carruth, p. 20)

1652, April 30—"Virginia assembly elects Richard Bennett governor and William Claiborne secretary of state. Enters eight years of almost complete self-government." (Kull, p. 37)

1652, May 18—"First law prohibiting slavery by colonies in North America was enacted by Rhode Island." (Kull, p. 37)

1652, June 10—First mint in America established in defiance of English Colonial law in Boston. . . ." (Carruth, p. 20)

1655—"Lady Deborah Moody, Long Island, allowed to vote in town meeting, the one known instance of woman suffrage in colonies." (Kull, p. 38)

1656—"A library in which the public may read opened in Boston." (Kull, p. 38)

1656, September 22—"General Provincial Court in session at Patuxent, Maryland; empaneled first all-woman jury in colonies to hear evidence against Judith Catchpole . . . after hearing her evidence, jury acquitted her." (Carruth, p. 22)

1657—"The Scots Charitable Society of Boston for relief of poor established." (Kull, p. 38)

1658—"Plymouth colony adopts workhouse program, providing work for vagrants, rebellious children, and stubborn servants." An early example of Government Welfare. (Kull, p. 39)

1658, August 12—"First police force or *ratelwacht,* formed in New Amsterdam, consisted of ten watchmen paid twenty-four stuyvers (about fifty cents) a night. . . ." (Carruth, p. 22)

1659—"Latin School in New Amsterdam opened." (Kull, p. 39)

1659—Massachusetts introduces system of making each township responsible for its own paupers. (Doyle, Vol. 3, p. 51)

1660—"Boston establishes an almshouse." (Kull, p. 39)

1660—"First divorce case in Delaware involved Finnish couple. 'The wife receives daily a severe drubbing and is expelled from the house like a dog.' Husband was adulterer, and divorce was granted. . . ." (Carruth, p. 25) Until now divorce almost impossible in colonies.

1661, September 9—Suspension of Quaker Persecution. "A royal order which reached Boston, . . . commanded that all Quakers under sentence of death or corporal punishment be removed to England for trial. Massachusetts released all imprisoned Quakers, permitting them to leave the colony rather than sending them to England for trial, and suspended 7 December the corporal punishment act of 1 June, but within a year (18 October 1662) that penalty was revived." (Morris, p. 37) Example of the frequent defiance of a royal order.

1662—Massachusetts accepts the "Half-way Covenant," relaxing former requirements for church membership and ultimately weakening the domination of the state by the church. (Hofstadter, inside cover.) The Connecticut Colony procured an unusually democratic royal charter. (In 1687, Sir Edmund Andros, appointed British governor of New England by James II, arrived in Hartford and demanded the surrender of the document. Legend has it that the townspeople hid the charter in an oak tree.) (*NYT Almanac,* p. 251)

181

1663—"John Eliot completes translation of Bible into Algonquin language." (Kull, p. 40)

1664—Marriage by Justice of Peace instead of clergyman made lawful in New York by Duke's laws. . . ." (Carruth, p. 27)

1666—"Governor Nicolls of New York says of democracy: 'It hath taken so deep a root in these parts that the very name of Justice of the Peace is an abomination.' " (Kull, p. 42)

1666, October 11—"Massachusetts Bay colony refuses to send representatives to England to answer charges brought against her by the royal commissioners, who recommended annulment of her charter." (Kull, p. 42)

1668, May 25—"First representative assembly in New Jersey meets at Elizabethtown." (Kull, p. 42)

1669, July 21—"Fundamental Constitutions adopted, plan of government for Carolina believed drafted by John Locke. Substituted for Concessions and Agreements of 1665." (Kull, p. 43)

1670—"Virginia slavery act decreed that slaves who had become Christians before their importation were not liable to life-long servitude. This law reflected moral concern felt in America over enslavement of Christians." (Carruth, p. 28) In 1682 Virginia repealed this law because of a sharp decline in slaves imported after it was passed in 1670.

1671, June—"Plymouth passes her first school law." (Kull, p. 43)

1672, May 15—"Massachusetts General Court enacted first copyright law in American colonies, issuing copyright to John Usher, bookseller, to publish a new edition of *The General Laws and Liberties of the Massachusetts Colony*. Protection was for seven years. Penalty for infringement was a fine of three times the manufacturing cost." (Carruth, p. 28)

1675—"First printing press in Boston allowed by General Court, set up by John Foster, America's earliest engraver." (Kull, p. 44)

1676, May–July—Nathaniel Bacon declared a traitor for leading a band of frontiersmen against the Indians, without having a commission to do so. An elected member of the Council (of Virginia), he was arrested when he later tried to take his seat in the Burgesses. He acknowledged his offense and was pardoned and released. He then rose a force of 500 and led them unopposed into Jamestown where he forced the authorities to sign his commission. The assembly then "enacted a number of democratic reforms." (Morris, p. 28)

1676, June 10—"Edward Randolph, commissioned to report on Massachusetts Bay, lands in Boston. October 12, reports to Lords of Trade Massachusetts' undue independence of British authority and recommends making her a royal province." (Kull, p. 45)

1677—William Penn framed his first charter which provided for the separation of church and state in the Quaker colony of West Jersey. The "laws, concessions, and agreements" for this province also included provisions "in great detail for 'the common laws or fundamental rights and privileges' of the inhabitants." (Bailyn, p. 195; *NYT Almanac*, p. 53)

1678—"Culpeper Rebellion in Carolina led by John Culpeper against navigation act of 1672 and quit-rents." (Kull, p. 46)

1682—"Tobacco-cutting riots on Virginia plantations to raise prices in glutted market." (Kull, p. 46)

1682—Great Law of Pennsylvania adopted by the representative assembly. Among the provisions: prisons to be workhouses and reformatories rather than simply places of punishment; prisoners not required to pay fees or support themselves; religious liberty; no servant might be taken for a debt (for the benefit of the master—"that the means of livelihood may not be taken from him"); all children to be taught reading, writing, and a trade. (Doyle, Vol. 4, pp. 396–397; Chitwood, p. 255)

1682, September 28—"West Jersey grants Matenicunk Island to Burlington for maintenance of a school, believed to be first school fund in America." (Kull, p. 47)

1682, December 4—"First Pennsylvania assembly meets at Upland (Chester). Incorporates Delaware settlements with Pennsylvania; adopts a code, the Great Law; naturalizes settlers already there." (Kull, p. 47)

1683—"Increase Mather organizes in Boston the first scientific society in colonies to effect 'Improvements in Philosophy and Additions to the Stores of Natural History.' " (Kull, p. 47)

1683—The ill-fated "Charter of Liberties and Privileges" passed by the First General Assembly of New York. It contained outlines for a construction of the province and a bill of rights. (Bailyn, p. 195). Much of the act was given to "the organization and practice of the courts, trial by jury, taxes, land tenure and conveyance, decedent estates and inheritances, the free exercise of religion, and the support of a ministry." The assembly passed other acts strengthening these objectives. (Flick, Vol. 2, p. 102)

1685, May 15—"Chief Justice Nicolas More of Pennsylvania was brought to trial on ten counts in first impeachment proceedings in America. He was expelled from office on June 2 for having wielded 'an unlimited and arbitrary power,' but was later reappointed to high office by Penn." (Carruth, p. 34)

1687—"The Excellent Privilege of Liberty and Property, etc. by William Penn, published in Philadelphia; it contained text of Magna Carta and other English statutes on freedom and property." (Carruth, p. 34)

1687, August—"Massachusetts towns of Ipswich and

Topsfield refuse to pay taxes levied without consent."
(Kull, p. 48)

1688, February 14—"Carolina assembly refuses to accept proprietors' letter declaring Fundamentals of 1669 no longer valid. Colony on verge of revolt." (Kull, p. 49)

1688, April—"The Germantown Friends' Protest against Slavery, presented in Monthly Meeting is earliest anti-slavery document in America." (Kull, p. 49) This proclamation was aimed at persuading all citizens throughout the colonies to unite against slavery.

1689—The Revolution of 1689 in Virginia—"A struggle between the governor and the legislature. A list of popular grievances was presented to James II. . . ." (Morris, p. 28)

1689—Assault against economic oligarchy in New York led by Jacob Leisler, disgruntled German merchant, who seized power and held it until 1691 when he was captured and executed by colonial authorities. (Carruth, p. 35) *Harper's Encyclopedia of United States History* (1912), Vol. 5, indicates that this was a struggle between the aristocrats and the democrats led by Leisler. Leisler was "railroaded" to his execution when his enemies in high places got the governor drunk and forced him to sign Leisler's death warrant. Years later his name was cleared.

1689—"Glorious Revolution in New England succeeded in ousting unpopular Governor Andros. On April 18, an armed uprising in Boston forced Andros to surrender Manifests, listed grievances of colonists and justified rebellion. Andros was returned to England to stand trial for misconduct." (Carruth, p. 34)

1689—"First public school in America with such practical subjects as science and inventions, William Penn Charter School, founded in Philadelphia with tuition charged only to those students who could afford it." (Carruth, p. 35)

185

1690—"The New England Primer printed in Boston, about this date." (Kull, p. 50)

1690, September 25—"Public Occurrences, a printed sheet, comes out in Boston as first American newspaper. No second issue." (Kull, p. 50)

1690, December—"Massachusetts issues her first paper currency to pay soldiers returning from Quebec expedition." (Kull, p. 51) Perhaps this can be construed as the act of a people who assume much of their own independence, since the coining and issuance of monies is usually a reserved right of the duly recognized ruler, or ruling body. In 1751 Parliament passed the Currency Act which prohibited the issuance of paper monies in New England.

1691—New York General Assembly enacts "Rights and Privileges of the Majesty's Subjects" which was even more elaborate and explicit than the legislation of 1683 (disallowed for its "large and doubtful expressions"). This act enumerated the rights of individuals as "a series of categorical prohibitions on government" including free from 1) unlawful arrest and imprisonment, 2) arbitrary taxation, 3) martial law and the support of standing armies in peacetime, 4) feudal dues, 5) restriction of freehold tenure; also granted due process of law, trial by jury and—if Protestant—freedom of religion. (Bailyn, p. 195; Andrews, p. 35; Flick, Vol. 2, pp. 156–157)

1693—New Jersey authorized towns to levy taxes for the support of public schools. (Carman, pp. 118–119)

1693—"Power to initiate laws granted by proprietors of Carolina to its assembly as well as to governor and council." (Kull, p. 52)

1693, February 8—"College of William & Mary in Virginia chartered." (Kull, p. 52)

1696—"King William's School, provided for by Maryland assembly, opens at Annapolis." (Kull, p. 52)

1697, February 8—"William Penn submits to Board of Trade proposal for Colonial Congress, with representatives from each colony and a president appointed by the king." (Kull, p. 53)

1700—"First library law in colonies enacted by South Carolina assembly for support of library in Charles Town." (Kull, p. 53)

1700, June 24—"Samuel Sewall publishes tract in Boston, *The Selling of Joseph,* condemning the holding of slaves." (Kull, p. 54)

1701—"Status of American colonial women indicated by fact that six sat on jury in Albany, engaged for special duty." (Carruth, p. 39)

1701—Yale College founded. William Penn compelled to grant the "Charter of Privileges" which affirmed the supremacy of the representative assembly and gave Pennsylvania the most liberal government in the colonies. (*NYT Almanac,* p. 286; Andrews, pp. 36–38)

1704, April 24—"*The Boston News Letter* begins publication; first regularly issued newspaper in America, continuing until Revolution." (Kull, p. 55)

1705—"Virginia requires by law that an apprenticed orphan shall be taught by his master to read and write." (Kull, p. 55)

1707—"Francis Makemie tried and acquitted by New York court. This signals the end of prosecution of Protestant dissenters in New York." (Carruth, p. 43)

1709—"Quakers of Philadelphia, Pennsylvania, formed first private home for mental illness in United States. In 1751 it became a part of Pennsylvania Hospital." (Carruth, p. 45)

1710, April—"Free school founded at Charleston, South Carolina, by act of assembly." (Kull, p. 56)

1710, June 21—"Colonel Alexander Spotswood, governor of Virginia, arrives at Jamestown, authorized by King to extend right of *habeas corpus."* (Kull, p. 57)

1711—"Bookselling now flourishing trade; in Boston alone about thirty shops were doing profitable business...." (Carruth, p. 44) Indicates a literate public and opportunities for communications on a wider spectrum through the printed word.

1712, April—"Slave revolt in New York City. Twenty Negroes burned or hanged." (Kull, p. 57) Evidence that slaves in America did not accept their condition as willingly as many have indicated.

1712, June 7—"Pennsylvania passes law prohibiting importation of Negroes." (Kull, p. 57)

1715—Rhode Island enacts legislation forbidding any church from obtaining any revenue through compulsion. (Rothbard, p. 26)

1718—"Five hundred pounds subscribed in Boston for Christian instruction of Indians." (Kull, p. 59)

1719—"Founding of nationalistic newspaper, the *Boston Gazette,* by William Brooker. In 1741 it was combined with *New England Weekly Journal* and launched attacks on Stamp Tax. (Carruth, p. 46)

1721—"Cotton Mather and Dr. Zabdiel Boylston introduce inoculation for small pox in America, with epidemic in Boston." (Kull, p. 59) (Also see Carruth reference on this point.)

1721—"Governor's censorship of publications in Massachusetts abolished by General Court." (Kull, p. 59)

1721—James Franklin begins publication of the third American paper, *The New England Courant.* Unlike its two predecessors, the *Courant* was not primarily a journal of news and advertising. Lasting six years, it existed "to give effect to certain political convictions and to ventilate current topics." Opponents described *Courant* writers as "free thinkers"; the "Hell-Fire Club." Increase Mather, writing in the *Gazette,* called for its suppression. (Doyle, Vol. 5, pp. 228–229)

1721—"First smallpox inoculations in America given by Zabdiel Boylston in Boston. He inoculated his son, Thomas, and two negro slaves on the recommendation of Cotton Mather. Mather's slave, Onesimus, had previously told his master of similar inoculations administered by African tribesmen, and Mather urged Boylston to try the practice. Angry mobs stoned both Mather and Boylston homes when they learned of the experiment."

"Although conflict (over the introduction of smallpox inoculations) followed traditional lines of science against religion, Mather, theologian, found himself arrayed against such secular figures of science as Benjamin Franklin." (Carruth, p. 49) This was a daring move, and characteristic of our colonists. The man who seeks freedom is marked by a tendency to question all aspects of life and not to be satisfied with a situation because of tradition or because power dictates it be so.

1722—"Daniel Coxe of New Jersey draws up first published plan for political union of colonies." Printed in London. (Kull, p. 60)

1723—"Schools in each county provided for by Maryland assembly." (Kull, p. 60)

1723—"Connecticut trading company became first recorded commercial corporation in America. Up to this time, land companies, universities, and philanthropic enterprises were only forms of corporate enterprise. Colonial restrictions on distribution of currency and restrictions from England on local trade and industry served to inhibit formation of corporations in modern sense." (Carruth, p. 51)

1724—"First horticulturist in America was Paul Dud-

189

ley, who launched the Science with his study of fruit trees in New England." (Carruth, p. 51)

1725—"*New York Gazette,* New York's first newspaper, begins publication under William Bradford." (Kull, p. 61)

1726—"Poorer classes in Philadelphia riot in heart of town, tearing down pillary and stocks and setting them on fire. The governor declares it a riot and puts it down accordingly. Similar outbursts cropped up in city: in 1729 crowds broke into mayor's gardens and destroyed his plants; in 1738 riot ensued when administration limited fishing on Schuylkill." (Carruth, p. 52)

1727—"*Maryland Gazette,* first newspaper in Maryland, begins publication at Annapolis." (Kull, p. 61)

1727—Connecticut General Court passes law exempting Anglicans from paying taxes to support the Presbyterian establishment. (Rothbard, p. 25)

1728—"Benjamin Franklin demonstrated his belief in reason as basis of religious faith with writing of his prayer manual entitled *Articles of Belief & Acts of Religion.* Franklin subordinated formal religious doctrines to commonsense logic." (Carruth, p. 53) Another break with traditions which tied the colonies to the "old world."

1728—Massachusetts passes a law permitting Quakers and Baptists to refuse to pay taxes to support Puritan ministers on the grounds of conscience if they attended some church and pledged allegiance to the colony. (Rothbard, p. 21)

1729—Connecticut General Court extends immunity to Quakers and Baptists. (Rothbard, p. 25)

1731—"First circulating library in America established in Philadelphia by Franklin." (Kull, p. 62)

1731—Massachusetts unconditionally exempts all Quakers from tax payments for support of Puritan ministers. (Rothbard, p. 21)

190

1732—The Colony of Georgia is chartered with religious freedom to be enjoyed by all—Catholics excluded. (Rothbard, p. 111)

1732—"Almshouse supported by public funds established in Philadelphia, probably first in colonies." (Kull, p. 62)

1732—"First regular stagecoach service inaugurated in New Jersey between Burlington and Amboy." (Kull, p. 62)

1732—"Benjamin Franklin begins issue of *Poor Richard's Almanac* (1732–1757)." (Kull, p. 62)

1732—"*The Vade Mecum for America* or, *A Companion for Traders and Travelers* by Thomas Prince published in Boston, America's first guide book." (Kull, p. 62)

1732—"First foreign language newspaper in United States, *Philadelphische Zeitung,* founded by Benjamin Franklin in Philadelphia, Pennsylvania." (Carruth, p. 56)

1733, July 30—"First Masonic lodge, under regular charter, established in Boston." (Kull, p. 63)

1734—"Popular party wins aldermanic election in New York City, assisted by John Peter Zenger's *New York Weekly Journal.*" (Kull, p. 63)

1734—Jonathan Edwards led and preached 'The Great Awakening' in New England, a religious revival that emphasized man's sinful nature and torments of his eternal damnation. In his parish in Northampton, Massachusetts, Edwards lived a life of spartan dedication. His fame spread to Boston, bringing invitations to preach and print his sermons. The influence of his example was strong, especially among young people. In December, 1734, there began a series of conversions, emotional in nature, and increasing in frequency, which was felt throughout the country. From 1740–1745 the movement was at fever pitch. It was condemned as a disruptive influence by the more conservative congregations and by the faculties at Yale and Harvard but began a religious mode which

191

proved congenial to many later Americans and did add to social cohesiveness in a time of great uncertainty. (Carruth, p. 57)

1734–5—John Peter Zenger, editor and publisher of the *New York Weekly Journal* tried for sedition; his acquittal was the landmark in assuring freedom of the press in America.

Massachusetts unconditionally exempts all Baptists from payment of taxes to support a Puritan minister except in new towns which have no minister; they are still obliged to pay for the Puritan church. (Rothbard, p. 21)

1735—"Georgia trustees prohibit slavery and importation of rum in colony." (Kull, p. 63) Later repealed by Georgia trustees in 1735.

1736—"William Tennent establishes 'log college' on his farm in New Jersey to instruct Presbyterian ministers for frontier settlements." (Kull, pp. 63–64)

1737—"John Wesley holds Sunday catechism classes for children in Savannah, Georgia." (Kull, p. 64)

1738—Land regulations relaxed in Georgia; females permitted to inherit land. (Rothbard, p. 115)

1739—"Three Negro uprisings broke out in South Carolina this year. . . ." (On September 9 a band of Negroes set out for St. Augustine from Charleston seeking freedom, and slaying all whites whom they met along the way. Twenty-one whites, forty-four Negroes perished before they were stopped. A second insurrection at Stone River and a third in St. John's Parish, Berkeley County, attest to the drive for liberty by the slaves.) (Carruth, p. 58)

1740—"Massachusetts land bank begins operations, issuing notes based on land mortgages. Discontinued by Parliament, 1741." (Kull, p. 65)

1741—"Journeymen bakers in New York City go on strike." (Kull, p. 65)

1741, January—"The American Magazine, first magazine in colonies, published by Andrew Bradford in Philadelphia. Three issues." (Kull, p. 65)

1741, January—"The General Magazine and Historical Chronicle for all the British Plantations in America, Benjamin Franklin, Editor, begins publication in Philadelphia three days after appearance of *The American Magazine.* Continues six months." (Kull, p. 65)

1745—"Growth of literacy in early America spurred by founding of twenty-two newspapers between 1713 and 1745." (Carruth, p. 63)

1745—"First appearance in American periodicals of writings of Montesquiew. These excerpts culled from *Persian Letters.* Later selections appeared in *Boston Gazette* were drawn from his Spirit of the Laws, which had profound effect on final form of United States Constitution." (Carruth, p. 62)

*1746—*College of New Jersey founded. (Princeton)

1747—"Some of the first flags created in American Colonies were those designed by Benjamin Franklin to be employed by military units opposing attacks by French." (Carruth, p. 64)

*1749—*Philadelphia Academy founded. (University of Pennsylvania)

1750—"Probably first free manual training classes in America established by the Rev. Thomas Bacon in Maryland. Enrollment was open to all without distinction of sex or racial origin." (Carruth, p. 67)

1750—"A Discourse Concerning Unlimited Submission and Non-resistance to the Higher Powers by Jonathan Mayhew published." (Kull, p. 68) Along with James Otis, Mayhew led opposition to British Parliamentary measures against "the Americans."

1750, June 22—"Jonathan Edwards compelled to resign from his pulpit at Northampton Massachusetts, by action of liberal members of his congregation who opposed his emphasis on sinful nature of man. Departure of Edwards marked end in New England of 'The Great Awakening' which his sermons had sparked." (Carruth, p. 67) (see entry in 1734 on Jonathan Edwards for more on "The Great Awakening")

1751—"Significant economic theory propounded by Benjamin Franklin in his *Observations Concerning the Increase of Mankind,* which held that wages of workers in America must be high because of abundance of free land. . . ." (Carruth, p. 66)

1751—The Academy of Philadelphia opened. Franklin's original suggestion was that the school be designed to broaden education and give less emphasis to classic subjects. The money to open the school was raised by public subscription, a forerunner to today's community-wide United Fund drive. The same year Benjamin Franklin got another project going, the building of a new hospital. Franklin saw that his new technique for raising money must be modified for the hospital because the cost of the project was beyond the resources of private individuals. Franklin invented the matched gift. Government ran in two thousand pounds for the hospital but only after an equal sum had been raised among the citizens. (Hawke, pp. 91–92)

1752—"Biblical sentence 'Proclaim liberty throughout the land unto all the inhabitants thereof,' chosen by Pennsylvania Provincial Assembly as the inscription for famous Liberty Bell." (Carruth, p. 67)

1752—"Pennsylvania Hospital, first permanent hospital in America, opens in Philadelphia." (Kull, p. 68)

1752—"Philadelphia Contributionship for the Insurance of Homes by Loss of Fire established, first fire insurance company." (Kull, p. 68)

1752, June—"Benjamin Franklin conducted experiment with kite and key to prove lightning a manifestation of electricity . . ." (Carruth, p. 67)

1753—"Benjamin Franklin received Copley Medal of the Royal Society of London in recognition of his research. . . ." (Carruth, p. 67)

1753—"Practice of medicine regulated in New York City for first time. An ordinance required that 'all the physicians and surgeons and apothecaries in the province are to be licensed.' " (Carruth, p. 69) Further evidence of progress in areas benefiting the public.

1754—"John Woolman publishes *Some Considerations on the Keeping of Negroes Recommended to the Professors of Christianity of Every Denomination*." (Kull, p. 69) (Popular anti-slavery writer and Quaker preacher.)

1754—King's College founded. (Columbia)

1755, November—The Virginia royal governor, Dunmore, issued a proclamation establishing his "Ethiopian Regiment," promising slaves their freedom in an exchange for a secure situation in His Majesty's service. He boldly seized Norfolk. Out of many thousands only 300 slaves joined Lord Dunmore's forces. He was defeated at Great Bridge. The Americans were wasting no time in ridding themselves of this "monstrous traitor." Lord Dunmore was fortunate to escape the mainland and get his troops onto British ships. The Virginia Convention issued a declaration urging slaves to return to their owners within ten days with the promise that they would be pardoned. (Blackburn, p. 92)

1758—"School for Negroes established in Philadelphia. . . ." (Carruth, p. 71)

1760—"Great American Contribution to transportation was the Conestoga Wagon, which first came into considerable use about this time. Developed in Pennsylvania where roads were somewhat better than in other colonies. . . . She could carry four—six tons of freight." (Carruth, p. 73)

1761, February 24—"James Otis delivers fiery address before superior court of Massachusetts against use of Writs of Assistance by British customs officers. 'An Act against the Constitution is void.' " (Kull, p. 72)

1763—"Tendency away from strict Calvinistic approach to God seen in two published sermons of Jonathan Mayhew, *On Nature, Extent and Perfection of the Divine Goodness.* Mayhew turned away from conception of God wielding arbitrary power and characteristized by spirit of anger." (Carruth, p. 75) This may be seen as a significant contribution to changing man's thoughts on the power of monarchies who derive their authority from the divine right theory, and the idea that all authority comes from God.

1763—"Beginnings of a free Negro tradition in New England reflected in presence of 5,214 Negroes in Massachusetts population of 235,810. Most of them worked at menial jobs in shipyards and homes." (Carruth, p. 74)

1763, December 1—"Patrick Henry arguing in Parson's Cause in Virginia, challenges authority of crown to disallow colonial statutes." (Kull, p. 73)

1764—Rhode Island College founded. (Brown)

1764–5—James Otis publishes his "Rights of the British Colonies Asserted and Proved." The pamphlet war is on.

1765—"First medical school in America opens in Philadelphia. Later, College of Physicians and Surgeons." (Kull, p. 74)

1765—"New Jersey assembly appropriates 200 pounds for unemployment relief." (Kull, p. 74)

1765—"Term 'Sons of Liberty' first used in English

Parliament by Colonel Isaac Barre, one of the few English opponents of Stamp Act. Later that year, clubs formed in Boston and elsewhere in colonies called 'The Sons of Liberty' and, in some localities, 'Liberties Boys.' " (Carruth, p. 76)

1765, March 22—"Stamp Act becomes law, providing for stamps on newspapers, legal papers, pamphlets, playing cards, etc. Internal tax to raise revenue within colonies. (Sons of Liberty organize throughout colonies to resist enforcement of Stamp Act. Non-importation agreements adopted by colonial merchants)." (Kull, p. 74)

1765, May 29—"Patrick Henry attacked Stamp Act in Virginia House of Burgesses, declaring that only colonial legislatures could impose tax on colonies. Shouts of treason interrupted Henry's speech to which he made his famous reply: 'If this be treason, make the most of it!' " (Carruth, p. 76)

1765, May 30—"Virginia House of Burgesses passes five resolutions proposed by Patrick Henry denouncing Stamp Act." (Kull, p. 74)

1765, August 26—Incited in part by Samuel Adams and other popular leaders, a mob entered and destroyed the Boston mansion of Lieutenant Governor Thomas Hutchison. It was Hutchison who used his influence to obtain the enactment of both the Sugar Act and the Stamp Act. Although he opposed both Acts as injurious to British and colonial trade, he acted in favor of their enactment in the belief that Parliament had the right "to govern and tax the colonies as it saw fit." In later years he was appointed Royal Governor of Massachusetts and served as such from 1771–1774. (Dictionary of American Biography Vol. V., pp. 439–443)

1765, October 7—"Stamp Act Congress, with delegates from nine colonies, meets in New York. 'A declaration of rights and grievances of the colonists of America' adopted October 19. Petitions to King and House of Lords adopted October 22, to House of Commons, October 23. On November 1 the Stamp Act went into effect amid the tolling of muffled bells and with flags at half mast." (Kull, p. 75)

1766, February 13—"Benjamin Franklin declares . . . that Stamp Act cannot be enforced." (Kull, p. 75)

1766, March 18—"Stamp Act repealed." (Kull, p. 75)

1767, June 15—"New York assembly, refusing to fulfill requirements of Quartering Act, is suspended by Parliament." (Kull, p. 75)

1767, June 29—"Townshend Revenue Act imposes duties on glass . . . tea (etc.) . . . into colonies." (Kull, p. 75)

1767, October 28—"Boston town meeting renews non-importation agreement. Similar actions follow in other colonies to compel repeal of Townshend Acts." (Kull, p. 76)

1767, November 20—"Townshend Revenue Act goes into effect." (Kull, p. 76)

1768—"War of the Regulation in Western North Carolina, a frontier protest against tidewater control (1768–1771), begins." (Kull, p. 76)

1768, February 11—"Massachusetts House of Representatives adopts circular letter prepared by Samuel Adams to be sent to assemblies of other colonies, suggesting united opposition to Great Britain by discussion and petition." (Kull, p. 76)

1768, June 14—"Old South Church in Boston became scene of the largest mass meeting ever held in New England. Meeting forwarded petition to governor demanding that British vessel which was hindering navigation in harbor be removed." (Carruth, p. 78)

1768, July 18—Probably first American patriotic song, *The Liberty Song,* by John Dickinson, appeared in the *Boston Gazette.* It had just been published in Boston and was on sale at London Book Store." (Carruth, p. 76)

1768, September 22—"Delegates from twenty-six towns in Massachusetts, called by selectmen of Boston, meet in Faneuil Hall. Drew up statement of grievances." (Kull, p. 76)

1769, May 18—"Virginia Association of ex-Burgesses, following dissolution of the House by Governor, agrees upon non-importation of British goods." (Kull, p. 77)

1770, March 5—"Boston massacre: three persons killed, two mortally wounded, six injured." (Kull, p. 77)

1772—"Watauga Association, formed to govern area outside normal jurisdiction of any colony, became first independent local government in North America. Land was originally ceded by Six Nations to English in what is now Tennessee. Not knowing what else to do with it, British turned area over to an elected committee of five, who ruled according to the articles of Watauga Association." (Carruth, p. 80)

1772, June 10—"British revenue boat *Gaspée* burned by mob in Narragansett Bay where it ran aground." (Kull, p. 78)

1773—"Poems on Various Subjects by Phyllis Wheatley, young slave girl in Boston, published." (Kull, p. 78)

1773—"Mental hospital, oldest institution (government supported) of its kind in United States, opened at Williamsburg, Virginia." (Carruth, p. 81) Originally called Public Hospital for Persons of Insane and Disordered Minds, it later became Eastern Lunatic Asylum and is now called the Eastern State Hospital.

1773, January 12—"First museum established in American colonies at Charleston, South Carolina." (In 1915 it was incorporated as Charleston Museum.) (Carruth, p. 81)

1773, May—"Regulating Act, passed by Parliament to assist British East India Company, encourages its shipping of tea to America, subject to three penny tax." (Kull, p. 79)

1773, December 16—"Boston Tea Party. Boston citizens throw tea from ships into harbor. Charlestown, Philadelphia, and New York also resist landing of tea." (Kull, p. 79)

1774—*"Summary View of the Rights of British America . . .* pamphlet by Thomas Jefferson published, Williamsburg and London." (Kull, p. 79)

1774—"Connecticut prohibits importation of slaves." (Kull, p. 79)

1774—Rhode Island renounces slavery, prohibits importation of slaves. (*NYT Almanac,* p. 287)

1774, May 12—"Boston Committee of Correspondence recommends to all colonies suspension of trade with Great Britain." (Kull, p. 79)

1774, May 27—"Virginia Burgesses, meeting unofficially* at Raleigh Tavern, Williamsburg, adopt resolution calling for annual intercolonial congress. Copies of resolution sent to other legislatures." (Kull, p. 80)

1774, September 5—"First Continental Congress assembles in Philadelphia with Peyton Randolph president. All colonies but Georgia represented." (Kull, p. 80)

1774, October 5—"Massachusetts assembly, meeting in Salem, reorganized as a provincial Congress. Subsequently adjourning to Concord, elects John Hancock president and forms military organization of minutemen." (Kull, p. 80)

1774, October 14—"Declaration of Rights and Griev-

*The House of Burgesses had been dissolved by Governor Dunmore on May 26.

ances adopted by First Continental Congress." (Kull, p. 80)

1774, October 14—"Declaration of Rights, consisting of ten resolutions on the rights of the colonists, including rights to 'life, liberty and property,' adopted by First Continental Congress at Philadelphia, Pennsylvania." (Carruth, p. 82)

1774, November 17—"Philadelphia Troop of Light House, one of earliest revolutionary military groups established in colonies, founded. . . ." (Carruth, p. 82)

1774, December 14—"First military encounter of Revolution occurred. It was not the battle of Lexington . . . May: John Sullivan led a band of militia to Fort William and Mary, broke into its arsenal, and carried off a store of arms and ammunition. (Carruth, p. 82)

1775—"Words of *Yankee Doodle* written by Edward Barnes and set to old English tune." (Kull, p. 81) The music of a people is a good indication of their mood and attitude.

1775, January 11—"First Jew to hold an elective post in New World was Francis Salvador. A plantation owner from the 96th District, he served in South Carolina Provincial Congress. On July 31, 1776, he was killed in a skirmish, thus being the first Jew to die for American Independence." (Carruth, p. 82)

1775, February 1—"Second provincial congress of Massachusetts meets in Cambridge to put province in state of defense." (Kull, p. 81)

1775, February 22—"First joint stock manufacturing company in America established to promote production and distribution of textile products as 'American Manufacturing of Woolens, Linens and Cottons.' Shares sold on subscription basis at £10 apiece." (Carruth, p. 83)

201

1775, March 23—"Standing before second Virginia convention held in Richmond, Patrick Henry delivered his immortal speech against arbitrary rule of England, closing with memorable words, 'Give me liberty, or give me death.' " (Carruth, p. 82)

1775, April 14—"First abolition society in America organized in Pennsylvania." (Kull, p. 81) Carruth (p. 82) says this date: The Society for the Relief of Free Negroes unlawfully Held in Bondage, the first abolition society, organized at Philadelphia, Pennsylvania, by Benjamin Franklin and Benjamin Rush.

1775, April 18–19—"Midnight ride of Paul Revere and William Dawes gives alarm of British approach to Concord." (Kull, p. 82)

1775, April 19—"Battle of Lexington and Concord. British destroy military stores, retreat to Lexington and then to Boston. Beginning of War for Independence." (Kull, p. 82)

1775, April 19—"Siege of British in Boston begins, continuing until March 17, 1776." (Kull, p. 82)

1775, May 10—"Ticonderoga New York, taken by American forces under command of Colonel Ethan Allen." (Carruth, p. 84)

1775, May 10—"Second Continental Congress meets in Philadelphia." (Kull, p. 82)

1775, May 31—"Mecklenburg Resolves, adopted by frontiersmen of Charlotte in Mecklenburg County, North Carolina, declare null and void all laws and commissions from King and Parliament. (Kull, p. 82)

1775, June 14—"Congress resolves to raise ten companies of riflemen and sets pay for officers and privates for Continental Army." (Kull, p. 82)

1775, June 15—"George Washington appointed commander and chief of Continental Army." (Kull, p. 82)

1775, June 17—"Battle of Bunker Hill (Massachusetts) fought. Though American forces ultimately had to evacuate their positions, they demonstrated courageous tenacity while defending it." (Carruth, p. 84)

1775, June 22—"Second Continental Congress resolved to issue paper currency of a 'sum not exceeding 2,000,000 Spanish milled dollars.' It was decided that the represented colonies (Georgia was absent) should pledge themselves to redeem the bills." (Carruth, p. 84)

1775, July 3—"General George Washington assumed command of troops of Cambridge, Massachusetts, that were laying siege to Boston." (Carruth, p. 86)

1775, July 6—The Continental Congress makes a *Declaration of the Causes and Necessity of Taking up Arms.* Benjamin Franklin, John Jay, Thomas Jefferson and John Dickinson were among those of the committee given the assignment. (See Commager, pp. 92–95 for Document.)

1775, August—"Thomas Paine, editor of *Pennsylvania Magazine,* inserts an essay on females, early plea for under-privileged sex." (Kull, p. 83)

1775, November 10—"United States Marine Corps organized by authority of first Continental Congress. Later assigned as a component of the navy in line with original intention. It was separately organized July 11, 1789." (Carruth, p. 86)

1775, November 28—"American Navy founded by Congress, adopting rules for its regulation." (Kull, p. 83)

1775, November 29—"Continental Congress resolved that a committee of five be appointed to correspond with 'our friends' in England, Ireland and France. 'Committee of Secret Correspondence' was formed; members were Thomas Jefferson, Benjamin Harrison, Benjamin Franklin, John Jay, and John Dickinson." (Carruth, p. 86)

1775, November 29—"American Cruiser *Lee* captured

203

British brig *Nancy,* which was laden with guns and ammunition destined for Quebec. *Nancy* was later named *Congress* and was instrumental in forcing evacuation of Boston." (Carruth, p. 86)

1776—"Satire of political conditions that brought about Revolution was chronicle play, *The Fall of British Tyranny, or American Liberty Triumphant . . .* by John Leacock of Philadelphia. . . ." (Carruth, p. 84)

1776—"Virginia abolishes entail. Within ten years all states but two have done so." (Kull, p. 83)

1776—"Thomas Jefferson advanced plan for African resettlement of Negro slaves. Similar ideas were widely held in South at this time." (Carruth, p. 88)

1776—"Philadelphia Friends' meeting excludes those holding slaves." (Kull, p. 83)

1776-7—Vermont declares its independence, draws up the first state constitution that outlaws slavery and establishes universal manhood suffrage without property qualifications. (*NYT Almanac,* p. 294)

1776, January 1—"Continental flag with thirteen stripes raised by Washington before headquarters at Cambridge." (Kull, p. 83) Visual expression of the new independent identity of the colonists.

1776, January 10—"*Common Sense* by Thomas Paine published in Philadelphia. Converts thousands to idea of independence." (Kull, p. 83)

1776, March—"Charleston, South Carolina, set up an independent government under a temporary local constitution which was to be in effect until an agreement with England could be reached. John Rutledge was chosen president. Said to be the first independent government within the recognized borders of the colonies. It was this government which successfully defended Charleston against the British army and fleet on June 28, 1776, thus freeing the South from attack for nearly three years." (Carruth, p. 88)

1776, April 6—"Congress opens ports of colonies to all countries 'not subject to the King of Great Britain,' but prohibits importation of slaves." (Kull, p. 84)

1776, April 12—"Provincial Congress of North Carolina instructs her delegates in Congress to stand for independence, first colony to do so." (Kull, p. 84)

1776, May 15—"Virginia Convention instructs Virginia delegates in Congress to propose independence." (Kull, p. 84)

1776, June 7—"Richard Henry Lee, chairman of Virginia delegation, offers resolution in Congress 'That these United Colonies are and of right ought to be free and independent states,' and that a plan of confederation be submitted to the several colonies." (Kull, p. 84)

1776, June 10—"Pierre Caron de Beaumarchais arranges French loan to Americans. Consent to loan obtained from Louis XVI by Comte de Vergennes in May." First formal act of foreign recognition. (Kull, p. 84)

1776, June 11—"Committee to draft a declaration of independence appointed by Congress, Thomas Jefferson, Chairman." (Kull, p. 84)

1776, June 12—"Virginia Bill of Rights drafted by George Mason, as part of Virginia constitution, adopted by Virginia Convention." (Kull, p. 84)

1776, July 2—"New Jersey first colony to grant woman suffrage. This statute remained in force until 1807, when it was reversed." (Carruth, p. 88)

1776, July 2—"Lee's resolution declaring independence adopted by Congress." (Kull, p. 85)

1776, July 4—"Declaration of Independence, as drafted by Jefferson and amended, adopted by Congress. . . ." (Kull, p. 85)

205

1776, July 4—"Jefferson wrote and rewrote the Declaration. He explained that he made no attempt at originality of principle. He simply harmonized the sentiments of the day in the briefest, most lucid way possible, although 'it was intended to be an expression of the American mind.' Still, the final document was a finely honed symbol of unanimity, towering above narrow regional rights, its theme fluid and strong though condensed, comprehensive in less than fifteen hundred words, vital in its philosophy of civilized freedom, focusing the vision of mankind's greatest minds. But the miracle was that it was adopted, not merely by a majority, but by all of the American colonies: The unanimous Declaration of the thirteen united States of America." (Balckburn, p. 97) Jefferson's most original contribution was the use of the term "happiness" in the phrase, "life, liberty and the pursuit of happiness."

1776, July 4 (afternoon)—The Printing Committee left the Continental Congress after final approval of the Declaration of Independence for John Dunlap's Printing Shop, carrying along various drafts of the document, including the eighty-eight changes made during the three-day debate. Minor changes are made as the type is set for printing. Approximately eighty to one hundred copies are printed by the early morning hours of July 5, 1776.

1776, July 5—One of the original printed copies is affixed with sealing wax to space left in Journal of Congress minutes for July 4. (This copy is on display in the Archives in Washington, D.C., on the immediate left after entering.)

1776, July 8—The Declaration of Independence was read to a cheering public in Philadelphia. The response was overwhelmingly favorable.

1776, July 9—The Declaration of Independence was read by George Washington to his troops in New York in front of the Federal Building. As throughout the colonies, the response was enthusiastically favorable.

1776, July 9—A New York crowd overturns the equestrian statue of King George III on the Bowling Green. (Freeman, p. 134)

1776, July 13—"Opposition to all titles in America spearheaded by Pennsylvania *Evening Post.*" (Carruth, p. 85)

1776, July 19—A professional penman, Timothy Matlack, was hired by Congress to write the Declaration of Independence on parchment to be returned to Congress for personal signatures of all delegates. Matlack used the printed copy as the text.

1776, August 2—The Timothy Matlack handwritten copy was returned to Congress for signing by those delegates present (approximately two-thirds of the fifty-six eventual signers were present and signed that day.)

1776, August 27—"Battle of Long Island. Patriots under General Israel Putnam defeated by General Howe." (Kull, p. 85)

1776, August 29—"Washington retreats during night from Long Island to New York City." (Kull, p. 85)

1776, September—"Benjamin Franklin chosen by Congress to represent the United States in negotiations with France for a Treaty of Commerce." (Carruth, p. 88)

1776, September 15—Washington's troops, stationed at Kip's Bay to repulse a British landing, retreat in the face of a superior force to the heights of Harlem. (Hughes, pp. 480–484)

1776, September 16—Washington's troops repulse the British on Harlem Heights and prepare new fortifications there. This action is known as the Battle of Kip's Hill. It was the first victory of Washington over the British. (Morris, p. 93)

1776, September 22—"Captain Nathan Hale of Con-

207

necticut executed by British in New York. Before he was hanged he made his famous statement: "I only regret that I have but one life to lose for my country." (Carruth, p. 88)

1776, December 26—"Washington captured nearly 1,000 mercenary Hessian troops in famous early morning raid on Trenton, New Jersey." (Carruth, p. 89)

1778, Winter through June 19—Washington writes to Congress chastising that body for inaction on behalf of the cause of Independence. (Hughes, Ch. XXVII)

1781, October 19—The war lasted five years. France joined as an indispensable ally. Then the end came when the siege of Yorktown ends with Cornwallis' surrender and 7,000 British soldiers become prisoners of war." (Kull, p. 93)

1781—Through the prior five years various additional delegates absent on August 2 signed when in the Philadelphia neighborhood. In 1781 the matter was declared closed. Several who were present on July 4 were never able to sign. Several others declined because they had opposed the Declaration of Independence but were overruled by the majority of their own state delegations.

In the final vote on July 4, New York had abstained because of lack of authority without specific approval of the state legislature. Prior to August 2 this approval was formalized, and, in the handwritten version, the word "unanimous" was added to reflect total agreement of all the colonies.

The printed version is headed, "In Congress July 4, 1776 a Declaration by the Representatives of the United States of America in General Congress Assembled." The handwritten version is headed, "In Congress July 4, 1776 the Unanimous Declaration of the Thirteen United States of America." It was in this document for the first time that the term "United States of America" was used to describe the North American colonies.

1788, July 2—". . . the President of Congress, Cyrus Griffin, announced that the Constitution had been satisfied by the requisite 9 states." (Morris, p. 120)

1789, April 30—"George Washington inaugurated at New York as first president of U.S." (Kull, p. 102)

Appendix I

The complete original text
of
The Declaration of
Independence

In CONGRESS, July 4, 1776.
A DECLARATION
By the REPRESENTATIVES of the
UNITED STATES OF AMERICA,
In GENERAL CONGRESS assembled.

When in the course of human events, it becomes necessary for one people to dissolve the political bands which
have connected them with another, and to assume among
the powers of the earth the separate and equal station to
which the Laws of Nature and of Nature's God entitle
them, a decent respect to the opinions of mankind requires
that they should declare the causes which impel them to
the separation.

We hold these truths to be self-evident, that all men are
created equal, that they are endowed by their Creator with
certain unalienable rights, that among these are life, liberty,
and the pursuit of happiness. That to secure these rights,
governments are instituted among men, deriving their just
powers from the consent of the governed. That whenever
any form of government becomes destructive of these ends,
it is the right of the people to alter or to abolish it, and to
institute new government, laying its foundation on such
principles and organizing its powers in such form, as to
them shall seem most likely to effect their safety and happiness. Prudence, indeed, will dictate that governments long
established should not be changed for light and transient
causes; and accordingly all experience hath shown, that

mankind are more disposed to suffer, while evils are sufferable, than to right themselves by abolishing the forms to which they are accustomed. But when a long train of abuses and usurpations, pursuing invariably the same object evinces a design to reduce them under absolute despotism, it is their right, it is their duty, to throw off such government, and to provide new guards for their future security. Such has been the patient sufferance of these Colonies; and such is now the necessity which constrains them to alter their former systems of government. The history of the present King of Great Britain is a history of repeated injuries and usurpations, all having in direct object the establishment of an absolute tyranny over these States. To prove this, let facts be submitted to a candid world.

He has refused his assent to laws, the most wholesome and necessary for the public good.

He has forbidden his Governors to pass laws of immediate and pressing importance, unless suspended in their operation till his assent should be obtained; and when so suspended, he has utterly neglected to attend to them.

He has refused to pass other laws for the accommodation of large districts of people, unless those people would relinquish the right of representation in the legislature, a right inestimable to them and formidable to tyrants only.

He has called together legislative bodies at places unusual, uncomfortable, and distant from the depository of their public records, for the sole purpose of fatiguing them into compliance with his measures.

He has dissolved representative houses repeatedly, for opposing with manly firmness his invasions on the rights of the people.

He has refused for a long time, after such dissolutions, to cause others to be elected; whereby the legislative powers, incapable of annihilation, have returned to the people at large for their exercise; the State remaining in the meantime exposed to all the dangers of invasion from without and convulsions within.

He has endeavoured to prevent the population of these States, for that purpose obstructing the laws for naturalization of foreigners; refusing to pass others to encourage their migration hither, and raising the conditions of new appropriations of lands.

He has obstructed the administration of justice, by refusing his assent to laws for establishing judiciary powers.

He has made judges dependent on his will alone, for the tenure of their offices, and the amount and payment of their salaries.

He has erected a multitude of new offices, and sent hither swarms of officers to harass our people, and eat out their substance.

He has kept among us, in times of peace, standing armies without the consent of our legislatures.

He has affected to render the military independent of and superior to the civil power.

He has combined with others to subject us to a jurisdiction foreign to our constitution, and unacknowledged by our laws; giving his assent to their acts of pretended legislation:

For quartering large bodies of armed troops among us:

For protecting them, by a mock trial, from punishment for any murders which they should commit on the inhabitants of these States:

For cutting off our trade with all parts of the world:

For imposing taxes on us without our consent:

For depriving us in many cases of the benefits of trial by jury:

For transporting us beyond seas to be tried for pretended offences:

For abolishing the free system of English laws in a neighbouring Province, establishing therein an arbitrary government, and enlarging its boundaries so as to render it at once an example and fit instrument for introducing the same absolute rule into these Colonies:

For taking away our Charters, abolishing our most valuable laws, and altering fundamentally the forms of our governments:

For suspending our own Legislatures, and declaring themselves invested with power to legislate for us in all cases whatsoever.

He has abdicated government here, by declaring us out of his protection and waging war against us.

He has plundered our seas, ravaged our coasts, burnt our towns, and destroyed the lives of our people.

He is at this time transporting large armies of foreign mercenaries to compleat the works of death, desolation, and tyranny, already begun with circumstances of cruelty and perfidy scarcely paralleled in the most barbarous ages, and totally unworthy the head of a civilized nation.

He has constrained our fellow citizens taken captive on the high seas to bear arms against their country, to become the executioners of their friends and brethren, or to fall themselves by their hands.

He has excited domestic insurrections amongst us, and has endeavoured to bring on the inhabitants of our frontiers the merciless Indian savages, whose known rule of warfare is an undistinguished destruction of all ages, sexes, and conditions.

In every stage of these oppressions we have petitioned for redress in the most humble terms: our repeated petitions have been answered only by repeated injury. A prince whose character is thus marked by every act which may define a tyrant, is unfit to be the ruler of a free people.

Nor have we been wanting in attention to our British brethren. We have warned them from time to time of attempts by their Legislature to extend an unwarrantable jurisdiction over us. We have reminded them of the circumstances of our emigration and settlement here. We have appealed to their native justice and magnanimity, and we have conjured them by the ties of our common kindred to disavow these usurpations, which would inevitably interrupt our connections and correspondence. They too have been deaf to the voice of justice and of consanguinity. We must, therefore, acquiesce in the necessity, which denounces our separation, and hold them, as we hold the rest of mankind, enemies in war, in peace friends.

We, therefore, the Representatives of the United States of America, in General Congress assembled, appealing to the Supreme Judge of the world for the rectitude of our intentions, do, in the name, and by authority of the good people of these Colonies, solemnly publish and declare, That these United Colonies are, and of right ought to be Free and Independent States; that they are absolved from all allegiance to the British Crown, and that all political connection between them and the State of Great Britain is and ought to be totally dissolved; and that as Free and Independent States they have full power to levy war, conclude peace, contract alliances, establish commerce, and to do all other acts and things which independent States may of right do. And for the support of this declaration, with a firm reliance on the protection of Divine Providence, we mutually pledge to each other our lives, our fortunes and our sacred honor.

Signed by ORDER and in BEHALF of the CONGRESS,
JOHN HANCOCK, PRESIDENT.

ATTEST,
CHARLES THOMSON, SECRETARY.
PHILADELPHIA: PRINTED BY JOHN DUNLAP.

Appendix II

Bibliography

Appendix II

Bibliography

Adams, Thomas R. *American Independence: The Growth of an Idea.* Providence, R.I.: Brown University Press, 1965.

Andrews, Charles M. *The Colonial Background of the American Revolution.* New Haven, Conn.: Yale University Press, 1924.

Bailyn, Bernard. *The Ideological Origins of the American Revolution.* Cambridge, Mass.: The Belknap Press of Harvard University Press, 1967.

Bailyn, Bernard, et al. *The Great Republic.* Boston, Mass.: Little, Brown and Company, 1977.

Becker, Carl. *Beginnings of the American People.* New York: Houghton Mifflin and Company, 1915.

Blackburn, Joyce. *George Wythe of Williamsburg.* New York: Harper & Row, 1975.

Boyd, Julian P. *The Declaration of Independence: The*

221

Evolution of the Text. Princeton, N.J.: Princeton University Press, 1945.

Carman, Henry J. *Social and Economic History of the United States.* Vol. I. New York: D.C. Heath and Company, 1930.

Carroll, Charles. *Rhode Island; Three Centuries of Democracy.* Vol. I. New York: Lewis Historical Publishing Company, 1932.

Carruth, Gorton and Assocs., ed. *The Encylopedia of American Facts and Dates.* Fourth Edition. New York: Thomas Y. Crowell Co. Inc., 1966.

Chalmers, George. *An Introduction to the History of the Revolt of the American Colonies.* Vol. I. Boston, Mass.: James Munroe and Company, 1845.

Chitwood, Oliver P. *A History of Colonial America.* Second Edition. New York: Harper & Bros., 1948.

Commager, Henry Steele, ed. *Documents of American History.* New York: Appleton-Century-Crofts, 1973.

Doyle, J. A. *English Colonies in America.* New York: Henry Holt and Company, 1907.

Dozer, Donald Marquand. *Portrait of a Free State: A History of Maryland.* Cambridge, Md.: Tidewater Publishers, 1976.

Fisher, George P. *The Colonial Era.* New York: Charles Scribner's Sons, 1901.

Flick, Alexander C., ed. *History of the State of New York.* New York: Columbia University Press, 1933.

Freeman, Douglas Southall. *George Washington.* New York: Charles Scribner's Sons, 1951.

Goff, Frederick R. *The John Dunlap Broadside: The First Printing of the Declaration of Independence.* Washington, D.C.: Library of Congress, 1976.

Hawke, David Freeman. *Franklin.* New York: Harper & Row, 1976.

Hofstadter, Richard, et al. *The United States: The History of a Republic.* Englewood Cliffs, N.J.: Prentice Hall, 1957.

Hughes, Rupert. *George Washington 1762–1777.* New York: William Morrow & Company, 1927.

Hughes, Rupert. *George Washington 1777–1781.* New York: William Morrow & Company, 1930.

Johnson, Allen, ed. *Dictionary of American Biography.* New York: Charles Scribner's Sons, 1957.

Kull, Irving S. and Nell M. *A Chronological Encyclopedia of American History.* New York: Popular Library, Eagle Books, 1969.

Lossing, Benson John. *Harper's Encyclopedia of United States History.* New York: Harper & Bros., 1912.

Morris, Richard B., ed. *Encyclopedia of American History.* New York: Harper & Bros., 1961.

Rothbard, Murray N. *Conceived in Liberty.* Vol. II, New Rochelle, N.Y.: Arlington House Inc., 1975.

Wright, Louis B., et al. *The Democratic Experience.* Chicago, Ill.: Scott, Foresman and Company, 1963.

Dictionary of American Biography. Vol. I. Edited by Dumas Maline. New York: Charles Scribner's Sons, 1961.

Dictionary of American History. Editorial Board. New York: Charles Scribner's Sons, 1976.

The National Cyclopedia of American Biography. Ann Arbor, Mich.: Xerox University Microfilms, 1967.

The New York Times Encyclopedia Almanac 1970: "An Outline of United States History." New York: The New York Times Book and Educational Division, 1969.

Appendix III

The Declaration of Independence

Census of Copies

There are only twenty-one known and recorded copies of the Dunlap edition in existence today. The following is a list of their ownership.

1. Harvard University, Houghton Library, Cambridge, Massachuseetts
2. Massachusetts Historical Society, Boston, Massachu setts
3. Yale University, Beinecke Rare Book & Manuscript Library, New Haven, Connecticut
4. New York Historical Society, New York, New York
5. New York Public Library, New York, New York
6. American Philosophical Society, Philadelphia, Pennsylvania
7. Historical Society of Pennsylvania, Philadelphia, Pennsylvania
8. Independence National Historical Park, Philadelphia, Pennsylvania
9. Maryland Historical Society, Baltimore, Maryland
10. Library of Congress, Washington, D.C. (Rare Book and Special Collections Division)
11. Library of Congress, Washington, D.C. (Manuscript Division)
12. National Archives and Records Service, Washington, D.C.
13. Indiana University, Lilly Library, Bloomington, Indiana

14. University of Virginia, Alderman Library, Charlottesville, Virginia
15. Public Record Office, London, England (Admiralty Records)
16. Public Record Office, London, England (Colonial Office 5)
17. William H. Scheide, Scheide Library, Princeton, New Jersey
18. Ira G. Corn, Jr., and Joseph P. Driscoll, Dallas, Texas (Leary copy)
19. Anonymous, New York, New York
20. Chew Family, Philadelphia, Pennsylvania
21. Kenneth Nebenzahl, Chicago, Illinois, and Hans P. Kraus, New York, New York (This copy is now owned by the Chicago Historical Society, Chicago, Illinois.)

ABOUT THE AUTHOR

IRA G. CORN, JR., grew up in Little Rock, Arkansas, and attended Little Rock Junior College. He served in the U.S. Army in World War II. He graduated from the University of Chicago in 1948 with AB and MBA degrees. He then joined the faculty of Southern Methodist University in Dallas as assistant professor. In 1954 he entered private business as a management and financial consultant.

His family background, which provided him with an appreciation for literature and history, combined with his education and experience, increased his interest in personal freedom, particularly as it pertains to America's economic system.

In 1969 Mr. Corn, in association with Dallas attorney and investor, Joseph P. Driscoll, purchased a rare copy of the Declaration of Independence which had been printed by John Dunlap in Philadelphia on the night of July 4, 1776. The document, one of only a few original broadsides of the Declaration known to exist, went to the two men for $404,000 following an afternoon of spirited bidding.

Mr. Corn is chief executive officer and co-founder of Michigan General Corporation (ASE) as well as co-founder and director of Tyler Corporation (NYSE). He is a frequent lecturer on college campuses and before other groups regarding economics, business, and freedom.

He is captain of the Aces bridge team which won the World Championship in 1970 and 1971.

Mr. Corn writes a nationally syndicated newspaper column, "The Aces on Bridge," and is author of the book, *Aces on Bridge.*